# THE ULTIMATE
# Culture
## IT'S ABOUT DNA,
## NOT RESUME.

By Erika MacLeod
and
Stacey O'Brien

**TulipMediaGroup.com**

◆◆◆

# THE ULTIMATE CULTURE

"*The Ultimate Culture* is what all business leaders need to read today. MacLeod & O'Brien demonstrate how it is not about finding great employees; instead, focus on becoming the business where great employees find you."
- John R. DiJulius III - Author of *The Relationship Economy: Building Stronger Customer Connections in the Digital Age* and Chief Revolution Officer of The DiJulius Group

"Stacey's and Erika's voices come through with clarity, and the workplace they describe sounds exuberant, supportive, intentional, and unique. The book is an invitation to follow their lead and create meaningful culture in any organization. How many companies have employees writing books about how much they love what they do?!"
- Heidi Huettner - Chairman of the Board of OpenWorm Foundation and Founding Board Member of Gathering of Titans

"This book is a rare look into the internal clockwork. It's like peering through a window into how to make a company run smoother and boost morale. These ladies have nailed it in terms of company culture, and their enthusiasm is inspiring. Ten out of ten recommended for your next weekend read."
- Tony Lillios, Founder of Speck Products and Integral Coach at Tony Lillios (Aliva)

"You know I love any company that truly embraces core values and company culture. Well, Erika and Stacey have nailed it in their book *The Ultimate Culture*. I love how they describe the unique culture of Tulip Media, providing great examples and inspiration that all business owners can draw from."
- Darius Mirshahzadeh, Serial Entrepreneur, High Growth CEO, and Best-Selling Author of *The Core Value Equation*

"If we were going to thrive in business, we all needed to explore new ideas and challenge our minds to think outside the box. Stacey and Erika have hit it bang on in *The Ultimate Culture*. The power to change, recreate, and continue must and will only come from within. It can't be forced. It must be fostered, nurtured, and bred into the DNA of a company that understands its sole purpose is to succeed together so we all will get better."
- Jim Gilbert, Canada's Huggable Car Dealer at Wheels and Deals

"If a business is to grow and prosper, the corporate culture has to nurture a shared vision and team passion. In *The Ultimate Culture*, Erika and Stacey do a great job of laying out how Tulip Media has worked the magic of developing a winning corporate culture."
- Krista Ross, CEO, Fredericton Chamber of Commerce

"Every business owner knows that having a great culture is essential for growth. *The Ultimate Culture* will inspire leaders to intentionally design a values-driven culture, where everybody gets on the same page and pulls together. High-performance workplace cultures don't just happen by default!"
- Dr. Craig Overmyer, Cofounder of Cultures That Work Inc.

"A breath of fresh air to see stories told by employees rather than a researcher. Stacey and Erika are not just sharing their own real-life experiences but also provide simple tips on how we can do the same in our own business."
- Ron Lovett, President of RFL Group of Companies, Entrepreneur, Author, Speaker.

# CONTENT

# Forward

## BY ANDY BUYTING
### FOUNDER & CEO, TULIP MEDIA GROUP

There are few things I believe in more than a strong company culture. Culture is a defining element of any organization, with the ability to make or break success. In this regard, I think an organization's culture trumps pretty much anything else.

I was thrilled when one of our partners, Heidi Huettner, challenged our team to write a book. Acting and thinking like entrepreneurs (one of the five core values you'll read about in this book), Stacey and Erika stepped up and decided to become published authors. Together, they wrote this book, and personally, I could not be more proud of what they've created.

I think this is a wonderful story of our journey and our culture here at Tulip Media. Stacey and Erika have been able to share their insight with the outside world. As a company, we leveraged our own talent of publishing to bring this grand project to fruition.

I was first introduced to the concept of company culture—how to discover it, create it, and cultivate it—when I joined Entrepreneurs' Organization (EO) back in 1999.

When I joined EO, I learned a lot about business from my peers as well as various thought leaders. One of my goals in joining that organization was to be accepted into an education program called Birthing of Giants (BOG). This was a three-year program held at MIT's Endicott House in Boston. It was there that I met Verne Harnish, the founder of EO and facilitator for the BOG program.

Verne talked about the importance of company culture, which is defined through a company's core values and core purpose, or reason for being. That concept really stuck with me. I started to think about the culture I had in my company at the time in the retail home and garden space. Drawing upon Verne's teachings as well as those of Jim Collins, I remember coming back and writing up the core values for the company. Twenty years later, I still remember those core values, exactly as they were originally written. Those values were instilled into our organization and completely transformed the culture of my company at the time.

Over an eight-year period, that company grew to 125 employees, and each employee knew our core values like the back of their hand.

Steve Jobs says that your company culture is the one competitive advantage that your competition cannot take away from you. It cannot be replicated because no other organization can create the exact culture that you have.

Denise Lee Yohn, in her book *Fusion*, talks about how core values—designed to create internal culture—should be a direct reflection of your company's external brand. This "fusion" between core values and your brand creates total cohesiveness between your company's internal culture and its external brand. This is how some companies develop resilient brands that remain strong and constant over time.

A quick litmus test for cohesiveness between culture and brand was put forward by a good friend of mine, Ken Sim, founder of Nurse Next Door. He draws out three tiers to the question of who can define your core values. At tier one, can your leadership define your core values? At tier two, can your employees define your core values? And, finally, at tier three, can your customers define your core values?

Tier three is interesting because it takes the test to a deliberately higher level where you are communicating your core values through your brand. If the answer to all three of these questions is yes, this indicates that you have total fusion between brand and culture. I find this exercise very fascinating.

Another inspiration to me in the development of our culture was Jack Daly.

When I first met Jack, he challenged me by asking the question, "Is your company culture by design or by default?"

Every organization has a culture. Like an open field, you can either choose to cultivate a beautiful garden or you can just let it grow over with weeds. It's up to you. The interesting thing, though, is that you can create a beautiful garden, but if you don't tend to it all of the time, it will eventually be taken over by weeds. It is equally as important to nurture your culture as it is to grow it.

That's the analogy I use when I look at company culture, recognizing that an organization needs to create its culture by design and nurture it. Remind people, keep that culture top of mind all of the time, or else it will grow over with weeds.

I made the conscious decision after that day with Jack to create my company's culture by design and to not let it happen by default. Shortly before starting Tulip Media from the basement of my house, I landed twelve new contracts in one week. These were all with Client-Partners looking for the unique set of services I'd developed. Lo and behold, that was enough to launch the idea I had into a new business, but I soon realized the amount of work would be too much for just me. I prepared to hire my first employee.

Even though I was only a team of one at the time, I sat down and defined exactly what I believed my core values were. What were the things that I valued right down to my core? I listed five of them and went out to hire my very first employee. This led to a second employee shortly thereafter, then a third, fourth, fifth, and so on. My company was growing, and the best thing was that our company culture was by design, entirely based on these core values.

Our core values have evolved over the last six years, but the essence of them has stayed the same. Our core values remain centered around the company's original name, Carle Publishing (named by my then four-year-old daughter, who drew inspiration from her and her brother's names: Carter and Leah), when I captured those initial twelve contracts. Our five core values—spelling out the acronym C.A.R.L.E. and discussed in detail in chapters six through ten—inspired Stacey and Erika with the content for this book. Although we've since rebranded, our values have stayed true to our core and pay homage to our humble beginning.

Our five core values are very much alive and well inside the company. In fact, we review a different one every single morning as part of our daily huddle. As an organization, we hire, coach, evaluate and even fire people based on these five core values. We all recognize that we have created something special, and now we need to tend to our garden to ensure that it flourishes for decades to come.

I am very proud of this book, written by two of our original team members. I remember when I hired both Stacey and Erika (employees number 2 and 4, respectively). I tend to put new employees through the ringer with a grueling recruiting process because I want to ensure we're hiring the right people who will fit our culture.

I knew Stacey was the one when, after learning about my company, the values I had written, and my vision for the future, she essentially told me she was showing up to work on Monday morning, whether she was hired or not.

Erika was so invested in our company's culture and vision that during one of her last interviews, she asked, if she were offered the position, would it be too late for her to take part in the round of employee stock investments that we were closing shortly thereafter? She was ready to not only invest her time and energy but her money into the company as well!

Both of these ladies are incredible people, and I am so proud to have them both on our team!

# Chapter One

## THE DAY THE WORLD STOPPED

The office was alive with pandemic chatter. We had spent the week prior watching the news about COVID-19, and each morning we came into the office, the talk was about a whole new outbreak in another region. It seemed the ripple effects were making their way closer and closer to our homes and workplace in New Brunswick, Canada.

Day cares began shutting down, causing issues for the parents on our team. Local malls and other large gathering areas were being told to close. It all felt so surreal.

We began starting our day by sanitizing surfaces. It's hard to wrap your head around something like that actually happening. Suddenly they were calling it a pandemic.

We immediately made the collective decision to disperse and work from home. Andy, who had remained the voice of calm and reason throughout the onset, stayed behind and staffed the empty office.

We were officially separated and set up to work entirely remotely on March 17th of 2020. I will never forget that day. In what felt like just a few short minutes, we had packed up our monitors, laptops, and everything else we would need to work from home and left the familiar walls of our office workspaces.

It was a strange feeling, not knowing when we would see each other again or how long we would work this way. A week? A month? There were so many unknowns. How long could a pandemic last, anyway?

Little did we know, this would become our new way of working permanently.

Nonetheless, and just the same as we did every other day, we all joined in on our daily huddle at 8:47 the next morning to share our usual agenda. It was like we didn't skip a beat. During our morning huddles, we each go through our to-do list for the day, voice our "stucks" or challenges, and update each other on sales and leads, what happened yesterday, and what we are working on for today. We never end a meeting without reviewing a core value for the day.

We were at dining room tables with children, dogs, husbands, and wives in the background, juggling our way into a new work-life balance and piecing together very quickly what that should look like.

Previously, we'd had the option to work from home two days a week on Tuesdays and Thursdays, which helped set us up for a successful transition. Fortunately, this meant we already had the equipment and tools to succeed as a team no matter where we were. It was like we had set ourselves up for success prior to the pandemic without knowing it was coming.

As most of our Client-Partners are in different parts of the United States and Canada, we often connect with them remotely. Already having a dynamic understanding of what digital collaboration should look like from the development of our Client-Partner relationships made it easy for us to translate these practices into internal operations. Client-Partners too were working through the challenges on their end.

It was an interesting change in dynamic. We already had steadfast relationships with each of our Client-Partners, but in the wake of COVID-19, these relationships became more personal as we invited them to digitally enter our homes and get to know us on a deeper level. Likewise, we really got to know them and the lives behind our clients. They too were working amidst family and pets, husbands and wives. This change in pace cultivated a more human side to our working relationships, and it was such a treat to see this side of people we had seen primarily in a professional setting.

Fortunately, each one of our team had a subscription to Zoom prior to the pandemic. We'd actually been using Zoom for over a year, but the pandemic opened the door for us to really take advantage of all that this platform had to offer.

In the years prior, we had removed our office telephones and instead utilized the mobility of our cell phones. We use a great service called Line2 that provides the ability to transfer calls and do conference calling among us. This is specifically a business phone service that lets us talk and text using a mobile app. It adds a second phone number onto our phones, so our business calls are kept separate from personal calls and texts, effectively letting us carry the office with us and take business calls from wherever we are.

Although we were already very familiar with these tools for working with Client-Partners digitally, we had never used them internally. Suddenly, here we were exploring all of these channels again for interoffice communication, and it was working well for us.

We quickly learned the importance of good quality video and sound and using the appropriate lighting to recreate our professional environment remotely. So we brought home from the office our high-definition Logitec webcams and Snowball mics, which we use to ensure high-quality picture and sound during meetings with Client-Partners. This same hardware is now helping our team to stay connected, seen and heard from home.

Thanks to green screens, we are able to look professional in Zoom meetings with Client-Partners even if we're sitting at our dining room table in pajamas from the waist down (and, to be honest, we usually were). We have the choice between five backgrounds designed by us. This makes it so each person has the same branding and décor on their screen throughout company calls.

Some of us have collapsible green screens that pop up on a dime and can be stored easily. Some of us have one that pulls down and retracts back into the ceiling. It's convenient to be able to choose the background and change backgrounds between meetings if we like.

Finally, we transferred our company dashboards online so everyone could see an overview of what was going on from their home office in real time.

All of us dove into books, webinars, and online courses, working to educate ourselves as much as we could those few weeks when business was slow. If we were going to come out of this on the other side, we all needed to explore new ideas and challenge our minds to think outside the box. As a result, our team members each read a total of twenty books and attended several constructive webinars and online courses in that COVID quarter.

It was not all flawless. Just about a week in, we were sneaking back into the office to steal our office chairs and any necessities to make our dining room offices more comfortable.

After a few weeks of working so well in a digital setting, we decided to make the move online permanent. All Tulip team members purchased desks for their home office along with printers. We moved out of our leased office space and became an entirely virtual company. For those who live in town, we still meet Mondays as a group to keep the connection, but to work for Tulip Media now, you can reside just about anywhere in the world.

Business as usual certainly changed when we started to work from home full time. Client-Partners located all across Canada and the United States were packing up as well and relocating to their home offices.

The phone calls and emails from frantic Client-Partners started coming in as we'd expected they would, along with news that business had taken a downturn and company budgets had been cut. We reached out to help in whatever ways we could, but ultimately, we did lose a few Client-Partners to the recession.

We watched the COVID-19 pandemic unfold around us and struggled through the economic ripple effects.

Each day for about a week, there was bad news and more bad news. In one week, our sales decreased by 43 percent. For a short time, we were worried that we weren't going to make it. How would we get new clients to replace the ones we'd lost? Would there be a job to come back to at the end of this?

Andy's response to this was that we were all committed for the long haul and we were going to find a way to make it work.

**"Culture eats strategy for breakfast."**

– Peter Drucker, Author

# Chapter Two

## THE "NEW NORMAL"

---

In almost no time at all, we were settled into our new routines. Our calendar schedules remained the same, so we continued with our normal rhythm of meetings, only now they were all on Zoom.

Weekly, we would still have a tactical meeting, one-on-ones with Andy and each other, daily huddles, and the famous Beer O'Clock to keep us connected and on track. Of course, a downside now was that we had to buy our own beer.

Although the physical in-office dynamic was no longer something we could enjoy, we made up for it in other ways. The tools we use to manage business in the digital realm are extremely versatile, and we quickly made them our own with custom ringers, nostalgic images, a little note here and there, and of course, a whole lot of teasing. New inside jokes emerged from our experiences engaging with each other remotely and the quirks and chaos that come with working around kids, pets, spouses, and unexpected visitors.

It was inspiring to us how rapidly everyone adapted to the transition. It was almost like we had been meant to work this way all along. As we continued to explore the dynamics of the new digital normal, we began to wonder if we even needed an office at all. Could this become our new normal, permanently?

Even though prior to the pandemic, we weren't at all exploring the idea of a 100 percent virtual office, we were all accustomed to having the flexibility to work from home a couple of days a week.

Because we already knew what we were doing, transitioning to a virtual office really made the most sense given these unprecedented circumstances. A huge part of our culture is the ability to roll with the punches and embrace new ideas. No matter what curveballs business and Mother Nature throw our way, we are always ready to try something new. Above all else, we always do what's in the best interest of our company as a whole, so that's what we did.

Andy was ultimately the one to make the call to disperse permanently. Erika believes her "line of sound" into his office might have played into the decision, as he very often joked that instead of being in her line of sight, he was in her line of sound and picked up on all her chirps and chitter chatter while he was trying to work. Working from home means he is able to focus in peace and quiet all day long.

There was another side to working from home: it saved us a ton of money. We knew that, ultimately, COVID-19 would result in a global recession and that we needed to be prepared for that if we wanted to survive the aftermath.

Ninety percent of our Client-Partners are in the United States, so it wasn't like we needed an office for them to come to when we were meeting them via Zoom anyway. The branded green screen backdrops that we use now work just as well.

Our office space had been quite large. Too large for us, in fact. When we witnessed firsthand how comparable our success was while working from home, we really had to question this expenditure. In the virtual office, our productivity has skyrocketed, and although the office environment was not necessarily stressful, it is more relaxing to get work done in the peaceful home setting. It's difficult to justify keeping that fast-paced office space when all of us are thriving and more productive in a work-from-home setting.

With an already sharp decline in sales and the office rent being equivalent to the annual salary of one full-time employee, it made sense to explore other options. Andy's tenant was conveniently moving out of his basement suite right as we were going virtual, so Andy was easily able to convert the space into a dedicated home office for himself. As a CEO and business coach with two young children, having a dedicated space was still a must, but it didn't necessarily need to be far away from them.

The downside of working in a virtual environment has been the reduced social interaction between team members, which is why we prioritize physically meeting once a week. All of us recognize the importance of that physical connection to maintain healthy working and outside relationships. We've also made a point of meeting more outside of work to keep up with what's going on in each other's lives and seized the extra time working from home to get to know our Client-Partners better.

One of the little things we did to maintain our relationships with Client-Partners during the initial hit was to get acquainted with some of their children and pets. This was a totally new dynamic for all of us, and suddenly we were privy to firsthand knowledge about how COVID was affecting their day-to-day life. They were curious as to how it was affecting us as well, so this resulted in some great conversations and actually helped us develop new marketing strategies that could be more effective in this setting.

It occurred to us that we weren't the only company looking into being more flexible and exploring more work-from-home options. Many connections, Client-Partners, and other business leaders seemed to have the same idea.

Our new routines really don't look that much different except for the commute time, although working from home certainly does have an element of flexibility that working in a corporate office doesn't. Now, we are free to shower on lunch breaks and rearrange our task list around errands that need doing when it is feasible. If we need to go out and buy groceries during the day and it takes over an hour—no worries, no one is timing that. We all trust each other to get tasks completed on time, and we have collectively appreciated the added freedom and the reduced pressure of our virtual world.

The total trust we have in each other has empowered us for success in our virtual office. If we didn't have the mutual trust and understanding we've worked so hard to build over the years, then our transition would have looked very different, and it is unlikely that we would have been positioned for long-term success within this revised framework.

In order to successfully digitize our working relationships, it has been essential to know each person on the team is keeping up with their workload while paying careful attention to quality, ease, and return on investment for our Client-Partners. Thankfully, we are all so aligned with our core values that it's unlikely this will ever become a concern for our team.

With each project that comes in, we all know when that project will be handed off to the next person, and we trust the next person will be ready to efficiently take it on. We mitigate this process through daily huddles and weekly tactical meetings that check in with everyone and make sure we're all on track in our roles and assignments.

Our attitude remains that, as Andy puts it, "we hire smart people to get sh*t done." This means we don't have to babysit each other. No one has to micromanage. All of us have assumed a leadership role, and this is an expectation we would have of any new employee. This mind-set has really enabled us to succeed in a virtual world because each of us is so driven for success individually and knows that we would all hold anyone we hire to the same standard.

Pivoting in the midst of the pandemic came naturally for us because we were already so accustomed to working together toward evolving our company. When it came time to make changes that would enable us to survive the downturn, we, as a team, were ready.

Together, we brainstormed a revised strategy that would see us through the initial pandemic and the recession afterwards. We implemented those strategies as a team and continued to work together to grow the company despite the recession. The addition of SMarketing to our product offerings really empowered us as an organization, particularly because COVID saw many companies looking for an alternative digital marketing strategy as part of their new normal. We were really excited to see the direction our company was taking with SMarketing now at the forefront of our programs.

Throughout COVID, we had great success using the SMarketing click funnel systems we'd developed and really seemed to be getting pull from Client-Partners wanting us to create these systems for them. We had started dabbling and putting this program together just six months before the pandemic hit, so receiving a response like we did was inspiring. It seemed to be perfect timing for us.

We'll go in-depth with SMarketing (Sales + Marketing) in Chapter 12, but, in short, SMarketing is the use of online marketing and an inbound sales model to drive business growth. We started digging into this first for our own marketing, then quickly began to apply this digitized marketing strategy for our Client-Partners on a large scale.

Because we were able to utilize our own magazine content in all of our new SMarketing processes, incorporating SMarketing into our own programs was relatively easy and just made sense for us. Our development of these programs came about by our researching, comparing, and educating ourselves on back-end processes. Throughout COVID, we consumed as much material as we could find on these topics to best prepare us for the boom in business SMarketing would bring.

As we've settled into the new normal, SMarketing has opened up many new opportunities , empowering us and our Client-Partners to pivot to success.

We ended the mandatory stay-at-home with new sales, a strong pipeline, and an enhanced marketing strategy. The time we spent educating ourselves for success post-pandemic is paying off as we continue to drive up sales for both ourselves and our Client-Partners.

Even though this program was accelerated by the pandemic, we believe its success was inevitable regardless. All things considered, it ties in so well with the programs that we were already offering, aligns well with the system of core values we have in place, and has incredible potential to create a strong return on investment for Client-Partners as it drives sales growth. When COVID hit, we did have to pivot to accommodate the new normal, but the core of our people and our values was always there. That's one thing we realized through the entire process: how important our trust and alignment  are to our organization's ability to succeed no matter what the world throws our way.

**"With a single, unifying drive behind both your culture and your brand, you reap the benefits of a focused and aligned workforce."**

– Denise Lee Yohn in her *Harvard Business Review* article "Why Your Company Culture Should Match Your Brand."

# Chapter Three

## HOW WE GOT HERE

Stacey came into the picture in June of 2013, but the heart of Tulip Media was growing long before that.

Prior to starting our company, Andy managed Green Village, which was a large and well-known garden center in our hometown at the time. Stacey would often go there with her daughter to have ice cream, watch the birds, and browse the crafts and plants. It was a destination to spend a relaxing afternoon in the greenhouses.

She didn't know Andy then, but she did know of him. She remembers hearing his ads on the radio all the time. He had a familiar voice in the Fredericton area.

While operating Green Village, Andy had started a magazine for the company. He sold advertising in the magazine to local businesses in the area with huge success.

As any small business owner knows, it's tough to compete against the big box stores. The magazine that Andy created and distributed to the locals set Green Village apart and fed into its warm and welcoming atmosphere. In fact, the *Green Village Magazine* became the idea for Carle Publishing. The name Carle comes from Andy's two children, Carter and Leah.

Stacey came to what was then Carle after having left a position she held for ten years with an employer that had a poor culture. She knew she did not want to go back into a company with a similar situation, so she put off accepting another job until she was sure it would be the right fit.

She ended up staying at home for a few months and catching up on some home maintenance before she decided it was time to start looking for a new full-time position. It was by no means a rushed process. One day, she came across a job ad online looking for a "rock star." After reading through the qualifications, she thought the ad must have been written for her.

Stacey had read through several job postings in the preceding few months, but this one really stood out. The language had her intrigued. Not only did the advertisement list the perks and benefits expected of every job ad but it boldly declared "This job is not for everyone" and went on to list some of the things that maybe weren't so great about the job.

It was an interesting way to position a job ad to attract the most qualified candidates, and she noted the strategy right away. For her, understanding the good and perhaps not so good about the position helped her to know without a doubt that she was the right fit because those discouraging bits were actually of interest to her. Ultimately, she knew she could handle all of it.

She later learned from Andy that this job posting technique comes from the Shackleton Ad. The famous Shackleton Ad was titled "Men Wanted for Hazardous Journey" and read as follows: "small wages, bitter cold, long months of complete darkness, constant danger, safe return doubtful. Honor and recognition in case of success – Ernest Shackleton." This ad ran in London newspapers in the 1900s and appeared at number one in the 1949 book *The 100 Greatest Advertisements* by Julian Watkins. Andy follows this technique in all of our job ads because it is a sure way to weed out any candidates that aren't a good fit. The logic is simple: if they are turned off by the downsides of the job at a glance, then it's unlikely they would be able to handle those aspects in actuality. In short, we want to turn those people off from applying because it means one less interview and less work overall for us.

Following the instructions detailed in the ad, Stacey sent in her resume and cover letter and waited a few days, then a few more days. She debated on calling, but was reluctant to upset a potential employer by calling their personal telephone. Finally, she couldn't help herself; she needed to find out more about this position.

It was just a quick call to introduce herself and let Andy know that her resume and cover letter had been sent to his email. It turns out this was the best thing she probably could have done to get her foot in the door for what became her position.

She followed up again with an email and finally got an interview. The interview took place at a local coffee shop and was relatively brief. Then there was a second interview.

She and Andy met at the local coffee shop again, but this time she was introduced to Carle's other employee. Andy invited Stacey to ask all the questions she wanted to about what both of them were like to work with and about the position itself. It was over a month and a half into the job application process when Stacey was asked back for yet another interview.

This time the interview took place at a local restaurant and took up the better part of an afternoon. By then she was thinking that if she'd made it this far, surely she would be offered the position.

Then came the assignments. After the assignments came the assessments. There were personality assessments and skill-set assessments. She hadn't even been hired yet and already she was being asked to work.

When she was finally offered the position, the hiring process had stretched into its third month. She told Andy afterward that if she'd had to go any longer, she would have had to invoice him for her time.

During those three months, she had also applied for other positions, but was thankful she'd chosen not to pursue them.

Stacey arrived on her first day of work to a small two-room office with only about two hundred square feet of space. The walls had been coated in whiteboard paint. Now she understood the coffee shop and restaurant interviews—Andy must have been worried the condition of the office space would scare her away! But it didn't.

Stacey's first week on the job was spent setting up the office to make it workable for the three of them.

At that time, we primarily produced Home & Garden magazines for the network of garden centers Andy had created during his time with Green Village. Our business model was to create magazines that were branded to our Client-Partners at cost. We would build our margins by selling advertising to national brands.

Of course, if we put millions of magazines in front of millions of consumers from a variety of industries, any national advertising brand would want to advertise with us, right?

Stacey had no previous sales experience but that didn't stop her from picking up the phone to sell these national ads. Turns out, it wasn't as easy as she'd thought. She had even tried calling the CEO of Coke, which is still a bit of a joke in the office today, but we do what it takes to succeed. It is one of our core values, after all.

Maybe we didn't have the national advertising that we'd initially expected in the magazines, but we did have a circulation of over 450,000 magazines, which is four times Canada's leading garden magazine. Those are some numbers to be proud of.

Taking a different approach, we decided to see if we could get in with some major marketing agencies that worked with the brands we wanted to sell to. I recall one agency telling Andy that if he was still in business a year from then to come back and see him.

We were three employees in a 200-square-foot office just trying to make a go of it.

Partners Tony Lillios and Heidi Huettner are in an entrepreneur group with Andy called Gathering of Titans. They became very interested in what we were doing and invested in our company. With that investment, we were able to expand our operations and decided to bring on a couple of experienced salespeople in October of 2013.

Undoubtedly, this would get us the attention of those national brands . . . right?

Immediately Stacey felt empathy, knowing all too well the rigorous hiring process these new salespeople would have to endure. Unlike her three-month interview process, the sales team interviews were accelerated and formatted as a group interview. The interview would take place in a room with five candidates all fighting for the same position at the same time. All she could think about was how uncomfortable these people were going to feel, but they all showed up!

Andy takes the hiring process very seriously. Each person had an equal opportunity to sell themselves for the two sales positions we were hiring for. Keith and Jay made it through the interview with flying colors and became our new salespeople.

After surviving the interview process, the two had yet to see the 200 square feet of space they would be working in. It had been tight with just Andy and Stacey, but now we needed to squeeze in two more? Somehow, Andy managed to fit two more desks into the tiny space.

Keith sat in the back with Andy, and Jay was in the front with Stacey. It was so small that if you needed to use the washroom, you had to ask Keith to leave his desk so the door into the hall would open. I remember Jay putting his lunch in front of the wall heater to warm it up. We were so frugal with company funds that we wouldn't even put up the cash for a microwave.

In 2014, Andy finally decided it was time to take over a larger space. We expanded into another available room in the same building and even invested in a small used microwave.

Not long after the team had settled into our new space, we were ready to hire again. Erika started in sales in June of 2015 and Jessica Embree started in marketing and design in August. Fortunately for us, Stacey's interview story still tops the charts, but we did need to jump through a few hoops to land our positions.

Although the interview process has settled down significantly under Stacey's helm, we still abide by certain formalities. Andy insists that we get a work sample before bringing anyone on board. Both Jessica and lead designer Carmen McKay were asked to do a small design project, which they both passed with flying colors. All our ghostwriters are paid to complete a sample article.

The interview process now consists of a quick introductory phone call with Andy followed by a longer one-on-one interview, then a group call when all of us jump on to get to know the person and answer their questions. As much as we are interviewing the person, we want them to be interviewing us to make sure it's a terrific fit both ways.

Besides the resume, we strongly interview for personality, work ethic, and alignment with our core values. We'll ask questions like "When was one time that you didn't give up and chose to stick with a task that really challenged you?" or "Can you talk about what it looks like to own a mistake and take responsibility for resolving it?"

There are usually a couple of in-office (or Zoom) meetings with several candidates before we discuss who would be the greatest asset for our team. From 2015 to 2018, we hired around ten people based on the DNA-not-resume methodology. Because of our culture and the way, we do things, some people have chosen not to stay long term and others we've deemed not to be a fit. We brought Carmen on in 2018, which is still our most recent long-term hire.

We went on to revise our magazine business model to become more profitable, opting to withdraw from our pursuit of the national brands. Soon, we were growing again. We hired a sales manager and three new salespeople, which lasted for the better part of a year. This was followed by four more salespeople soon after. We committed to this outbound sales model and even knocked out walls in the office to accommodate the new cubicles. All of us were shocked when Andy came out of his office one day and let them all go to pursue a new inbound model called SMarketing.

This change was our biggest one yet. You see, at Tulip Media, we embrace change because change is part of what helps us grow.

This time it was different. Andy had a plan to expand, but we weren't hiring. In fact, we did exactly the opposite. He decided we would no longer keep a designated sales team because we just weren't achieving the results, we wanted this way, contrary to what we had believed in so strongly when we'd opened up our office to hire these people.

The truth is, cold calling simply does not work anymore. Following the old "smile and dial" routine, spending hours researching business leaders to craft an email that would get their attention just wasn't cutting it for us. It was a tough decision to make, but ultimately the right one.

Back when we had a sales team, we used to receive around one inbound call a month looking to hear more about our services. All other sales calls were outbound cold calls originating from our sales team. Now, all our sales come from hundreds of inbound leads.

Seven years later, our company is bigger than ever and still growing strong. We are all exceptionally grateful to have the positions that we do and to work with the people we work with. We have created something incredible in terms of culture, service, and product offerings, and we did it as a team.

**"Customers will never love
a company until the employees love it first."**

– Simon Sinek, Author, Motivational Speaker
And Marketing Consultant

# Chapter Four

## OUR PURPOSE

---

Our purpose is a golden rule that all of us live by: to empower others so they can achieve greater business results through an Easy and Effective marketing strategy. We've been immensely successful in combining sales and marketing strategies to create the Tulip Media original program Andy has coined SMarketing. We focus our marketing efforts on a few key areas that we see as essential to generating quality business results.

First of all, we do all of the heavy lifting. What this means is that we take on the tedious, giving Client-Partners freedom to separate from the process while still reaping all of the benefits.

We put the work into making it easy with a seamless and supported process. Much of what we do is concealed in the back end, yet we are always working around the clock to make business better for you. If there is a way for us to make it easier for our Client-Partners, we jump right in.

The second piece is the creation of an effective distribution strategy. Driving results is essential, and we are committed to finding innovative ways to achieve this both internally and beyond.

Finally, we are committed to credibility. It is integral to our process that we are able to add value and expertise to marketing processes.

From licensed content to quality publications that educate customers, it's important to us that our Client-Partners walk away from every project knowing they've received an amazing product with a perceived value that exceeds expectation. We don't present anything as finished until we're proud. We believe each finished product should be a shining token of our company, and we work to make this translate into every single project.

SMarketing is a recent addition to this framework that has quickly moved to the forefront. To us, combining sales and marketing epitomizes ingenuity in business development concepts. We have had great success with this product so far and are eager to share it with many more Client-Partners to come.

In some ways, Tulip Media is comparable to a fairy godmother. We often find ourselves saying to Client-Partners in some way or another, "What is it you want to happen? Let us figure out how to make it happen."

If they want someone to be interviewed for their magazine, wonderful. We'll send an introductory email and take it from there. We have worked hard to be able to coordinate it all when it comes to articles, from interviews to imagery. We connect all of our writing clients with a ghostwriter who takes their ideas and transforms them into quality content for their blog, magazine, or other medium. All we need is that simple introduction to make the magic happen.

All of the legwork and everything "behind the curtain" falls on us. It's a priority that the processes for our magazines and digital content are easy to follow and come together smoothly for our Client-Partners. We do everything in our power to eliminate any stress and avoid confusion. All of our processes are constantly refined and always evolving to better accommodate inside and out.

Before ever engaging with you, it's common for us to research the types of articles on your blog or other content you are looking to outsource. That is just what we do and part of what makes Team Tulip such a joy to work with. We really do want to get to know you and your business and make sure we are giving you exactly what you need from us.

We want you to run your business as though sales and marketing are simply a small side project that we are coaching you through. We'll only ask you for a few task items here and there.

In regard to distribution, there are a lot of different ways to distribute both magazines and newsletters. Are you creating something that is mailed directly to your target customers, or will you be approaching local businesses? Your audience matters to us, so we will always tailor our tools to create content that is most effective for capturing the attention of your chosen markets.

For content being marketed directly to consumers, we take a nurturing approach. We will tailor our language and calls to action to whatever is appropriate and consistent with your branding. All content is based on who the reader is as a person.

For lead generation and conversions, the structure and verbiage of the articles will be noticeably different from an informational piece. We focus on making the article as efficient as possible for achieving its purposes, and we always do our best to meet the reader exactly where they are.

Behind the curtain, there are so many things that our Client-Partners aren't even aware that we do. These range from keeping on top of industry trends through in-depth research to the implementation of new tips and tricks for a more effective copywriting strategy. We are dedicated to always finding an easier way where there is a need for one.

We are also dedicated to accommodating the needs of our valued Client-Partners around the clock. Various applications that we use for better communication include WhatsApp, Zoom, text, and email. Some of our Client-Partners still like to speak with us on the phone. We're open to using whatever form of communication works best for you. Even if it is an application we may not have used before, we will adapt to you rather than bring in a channel of communication that you are not familiar nor comfortable with.

Everything we do is about saving time on your end, so naturally we want to make communication with you as efficient as possible and with careful attention to your specific needs. Communication with us should be effortless and make up a small portion of your day at most.

This is a form of building trust and one way that we gain credibility with you. Marketing with credibility is also of the utmost importance in our own SMarketing efforts. This translates back into the marketing strategies we've developed for our growing range of Client-Partners.

We utilize licensed content, which goes back to taking monumental pride in the quality of our products. In fact, we hold licensing for content created by some phenomenal thought leaders including Adam Grant, Mel Robbins, Gary Vaynerchuk, and Simon Sinek. Licensing provides us access to a large variety of content on many different topics. Pat Lencioni is one of Erika's personal favorites whom she reads and listens to often. The entire list of contributors is available with images and biographies under "National Contributors" on the Tulip Media website.

Providing your clients with valuable information is a great way to create quality content. If you can, pass along an article or idea from one of the greats. Simply sharing that information will help you gain credibility amongst your client base and beyond.

The magazines and the newsletters we generate using this licensed content—and more—feel utterly amazing when you hold them in your hands. They are designed to be on point with your branding, and we strive for your customers to take as much pride in the magazine as you and we do.

Doing business with a company that cares really shines through in a custom magazine or newsletter. That heartfelt communication is invaluable to your followers.

The SMarketing strategy that combines sales and marketing into a single, unified business development strategy is now at the heart of everything we do. At one point, we had seven business development managers in addition to someone that spent several hours a week just on marketing. We were able to turn that right around using the SMarketing approach. Now it's been over a year since our last cold call, and sales are growing more rapidly than ever before.

We have mastered the art of clearly and concisely getting a message out to everyone in just the right place. We strategically position our own message where potential Client-Partners already are, meeting you where you are just as we meet your clients where they are in the content we produce for you.

The combined sales and marketing approach that is SMarketing has performed tremendously well, especially considering the circumstances. There are so many components that just six months ago we weren't aware existed. A click funnel and search engine optimization were foreign concepts to Erika. Now everything she puts out is completely optimized for a target keyword or keyword phrase. We've come to appreciate to what degree marketing is a science, and the results of this shared understanding are really coming through on the other end.

Having existing Client-Partners come to us for a SMarketing strategy meeting, when they are already in the market for something else that we do, has been an amazing shift of growth and empowerment for us. We no longer have any salespeople beyond our dedicated back-end team. It is the production managers and those working in various other roles throughout the office that are tasked with interacting with new leads that come to us for information.

As production managers, we know firsthand the value we can offer to our Client-Partners. It is the people behind the curtain that know how the product and processes work. So that makes us the best people to explain it, because we can tell you exactly why it works and particularly why we know it will work for you.

When you approach us for SMarketing and more, we get to know you as someone we could potentially be working with for many years to come. This means we are going to tell you the pros and the cons and strategize with you about the tailored approach that is going to fulfill your needs and enable us to live Tulip Media's purpose: to empower others so they can achieve greater business results through an Easy and Effective marketing strategy.

"Culture does not change because we desire to change it. Culture changes when the organization is transformed; the culture reflects the realities of people working together every day."

— Frances Hesselbein, Former CEO, Girl Scouts Of The USA

# Chapter Five

## INTRODUCING TULIP CULTURE

---

Our culture is built on a foundation of mutual trust and understanding, dedication, drive, and constant growth. The culture that we've developed together is truly unique and wonderful, which is why we want to share it with you! We think going to work every day should be as fun and rewarding as it is for us here at Tulip Media, no matter what you do or where you're from.

Embedded in the culture here is a myriad of secrets for organizational success. You'll see that what we've created is special in that we operate effectively and holistically with an unlimited amount of freedom. Despite having few constraints, each of us is individually committed to seeing the company succeed. We all take our roles very seriously and are consistently mindful of the impact our work has on the organization as a whole.

With insurmountable team cohesion, we carry out our tasks each day with pride. The best part is that we're always cheering each other on. In fact, we're constantly on the lookout for our colleagues going the extra mile so we can be sure to reach out with a virtual pat on the back.

Creating the culture that we have today didn't happen overnight. It required a commitment to change and continuous movement. We committed ourselves to always acting in the best interest of the company, even when that meant taking a pay cut and making a full pivot.

Our company grew over the years from a small, 200-square-foot office with three employees to an office with more than enough space to accommodate seventeen employees to the virtual office we have now with an unlimited number of employees and contractors.

Since it would be difficult to keep up team morale if new team members were not promptly held to the same standard that we hold ourselves, a lengthy interview process is key to ensuring that each new team member we bring on is perfectly aligned with our values. This is especially important in the virtual atmosphere where we consider candidates from all over the world. We all went through a similar "initiation" process to assess if we were the right fit for our roles.

Later on, we'll show you what the recruiting process looks like from start to finish so you can try it for yourself.

Our culture extends far beyond the internal makeup of Tulip Media. The dedication we have to the company and to each other shines through in all that we do, including each new client-partnership we immerse ourselves in. All of our relationships with Client-Partners are enriched by the immense joy we find in our day-to-day work.

You'll notice that throughout this book and beyond, we refer to our clients as "Client-Partners." We have used this term since the beginning because we strive to build an equitable client-partnership that extends far beyond the standard working relationship.

The logic behind this terminology is simple. Our purpose is to become the outside force of your marketing department, working nonstop behind the scenes to bring your expectations to life. In exchange, we both reap the benefits of your success.

So much of what we do is acting as a sounding board. We take it upon ourselves to initiate those strategy calls when needed and use this time to really convey the knowledge that we have to you, for you. Whether it's designing a SMarketing system or tailoring our magazine program, we believe in this as a partnership, and it's important that this translates loud and clear into all of our Client-Partner relationships. We want you to use our marketing expertise to make your industry expertise shine through. That's why we're here.

Our client-partnerships can be as involved as you choose. If you prefer that we work for you from a distance, we will accommodate that too! Our culture makes room for everyone.

At the heart of Tulip Media culture are our core values. We see these core values as the roots of our success. It is our belief that avid alignment with these values is the secret sauce from which our exceptionalism grows.

We came up with these values together as a group, and as a group, we live out these core values every single day. Seriously. In fact, they're engraved on a plaque so that we never forget them.

In our old office, the values plaques were mounted in the entryway. Now that we're primarily digital, they're posted in the entrance to Andy's home office where we meet every Monday. When we made the switch to a virtual office, careful maintenance of our core values kept us all aligned and positioned for success.

Our values spell out the name C-A-R-L-E, which was the company name before we rebranded to become Tulip Media. Even though our name has changed, the virtues from which we've grown remain an integral part of our development.

When we say we live out these values every single day, we mean it. Better yet, we enjoy it because each of us wholeheartedly believes in the impact of our core values on each other and on our client-partnerships. It is impossible to forget the core values that make up the heart of Tulip Media.

We recite our values at quarterly planning meetings and at the beginning of our daily huddle each morning. We assign a core value to each day of the week in order. Monday is 'C,' Tuesday is 'A,' and so on. This is the same every week, so whoever is leading the meeting knows to ask at the end if anyone has a story that embodies the core value of the day. This encourages us to think back over the last seven days and examine where we've seen that core value in action, whether it's a big story for ourselves or recognizing someone else.

We make it easy to remember our values by using a Dr. Seuss quote to reference each one. This adds cheer and helps us to remember their significance. Without further ado, let us introduce you to the heart of our organization.

*C* is for **Complete Client-Partner Dedication.** Maintaining the partnerships we've built with our invaluable client base is paramount to us. Each partnership is unique to us, and later in the book, you'll find out just how far we'll go for our Client-Partners. From our expanding list of tailored program offerings to all of the little footprints in between, we are dedicated to always going that extra mile to achieve total satisfaction. Your success is our success, after all.

"And will you succeed? Yes indeed. Yes indeed. 98 and ¾% guaranteed!"

*A* is for **Act and Think Like An Entrepreneur.** A is also the first letter in the alphabet, which makes it number one. We respect that making it to the top requires us to think outside the box, and we strive to achieve this every day. We are candid with our thinking and always create an open floor for sharing new thoughts and ideas. In fact, we encourage each other to be odd. That's what makes us unique!

"You have to be odd to be number one."

*R* is for being **Relentless About Quality, Ease and ROI.** Our priority is always to add value and make working with us as easy as possible for our Client-Partners. We take it upon ourselves to do all of the legwork and commit to always producing a final product that we and the client are proud of.

"It's not about what it is, it's about what we can become."

*L* is for **Leadership, Teamwork And Open Communication.** What this means is that we understand each other's strengths and weaknesses and where we can leverage each other's expertise when it comes to problem-solving and collaboration. It also means we create open channels of communication with each other and an environment where everyone feels respected. We value the opinion of everyone on our team and are always receptive to receiving feedback and constructive criticism.

"Open your mouth lad for every voice counts."

*Ɛ* is for **Embrace And Drive Change.** We are incessantly enacting change in our company, constantly evolving and constantly trying to find ways to do it better. We don't shy away from being different because we've found a lot of great new ways to do things this way!

"Why fit in when you were born to stand out!"

Part of our holistic approach is that we don't reprimand each other when things go wrong. If a problem arises, we don't blame anyone or anything, we simply work together to find solutions.

All of these values empower us to be better and to grow in harmony with what they embody. As we continue to grow, we are working hard to keep everyone we work with in sync with the same set of beliefs.

Over the years, as our product lines have expanded, we needed a name that would best encapsulate who we are and what we do: a name that truly epitomized our core values and commitment to growth.

Andy's famous tulip jacket is what inspired us to choose the name Tulip Media. This particular jacket is covered in yellow tulips with a single red tulip standing tall amongst them. Against the background of yellow, the blooming red tulip stands out brilliantly. It reminds us to be willing to stand out against our competitors and be that red tulip in a sea of yellow, which we translated back into our brand.

Our Tulip Media branding is designed to seek out the red tulip mentality in a sea of yellow, to stand out from our competition. All of our core values align with this mentality, and each plays an integral role in differentiating us from the rest.

With the power of an unbelievable synergy on our side, we've built Tulip Media into an environment where everyone feels seen, heard, and appreciated. We believe in the power of this model with our whole hearts, and we want it to work for you.

**"An organization's ability to learn, and translate that learning into action rapidly, is the ultimate competitive advantage."**

— Jack Welch, Former CEO,
General Electric

# Chapter Six

## COMPLETE
## CLIENT-PARTNER DEDICATION

*"And will you succeed? Yes indeed. Yes indeed. 98 and ¾% guaranteed!" - Dr. Seuss*

---

The first of our core values is complete dedication to our valued Client-Partners. Establishing our client-partnership as an integral part of both businesses is essential to the strength of the programs and services that we provide.

We put the work into making it easy with a seamless and supportive process. Much of what we do is concealed in the back end, which is fueled by our dedicated team working around the clock to make business better for you. If there is a way for us to make the process easier for our Client-Partners, we jump right in. In the past, we have completely redesigned advertisements and covers numerous times to meet a client's standards.

Over the years, we have had some interesting Client-Partners, some of whom have been challenging to deal with and whom we've not been able to please. We don't mind saying this because if you're in business, your know that you've come across this too.

What makes us stand out is that we never give up on them. Once a project has been initiated, we will continue working to satisfy their needs even when it costs us extra money and extra time. We want to ensure that our Client-Partners are completely satisfied, always.

We may choose to not work with these challenging Client-Partners again, but we will not leave them without a product they are proud of. We honor our commitments, and we do what we say we are going to do, every time. Working with tight publication and printing deadlines, we need to have impeccable timing. We can't afford to miss a print upload date because, if we do, then we miss our distribution date, which would result in a late publication for our Client-Partner. Sometimes this has meant staying after hours and arranging for nighttime childcare so that we could meet our deadlines.

Jessica had worked every night for weeks on end to get magazines completed in time. For what seemed like forever, she was always the last one to leave the office. Her mother even delivered her supper many nights, and we all checked in on her. This just goes to show that we are truly dedicated to success for our Client-Partners, and we take our role in this very seriously.

During the COVID-19 crisis, we had a Client-Partner who needed a rush on their newsletter. This was because they wanted to get the newsletter sent out by the end of the month so it would hit the mail by the first of the month. This is an important time for landlords, which was the industry this particular Client-Partner was in. It was tough, but we knew that we could succeed if we all put our heads together and worked hard. We managed to complete the job in just four days.

We once had a Client-Partner with some disconnect between themselves and their ghostwriter. We had been moving quite fast with this project, and the writer was not quite hitting the points the Client-Partner wanted. In this case, our Client-Partner had a very specific vision for how they wanted the final piece to read, and our writers were struggling to bring this particular vision to fruition. This is not to say that the articles were not amazingly well written, but they were just not written in alignment with what our Client-Partner had in mind.

When the first iteration failed to meet their expectations, we immediately went through a second ghostwriter. Still, it was not quite what they had envisioned. So, we sent the assignment out to a third ghostwriter. Again, the articles were completely well written, but they were just not meeting our Client-Partner's very specific expectations.

What ended up happening is that we hired a ghostwriter the Client-Partner already knew and had worked with in the past. Finally, we were able to produce the articles that ultimately landed in the magazine.

We went above and beyond to make this exactly the fit that they needed. There were a few bumps in the road—as is to be expected the first time creating a magazine—but we were not going to give up and simply push these incongruous articles on the Client-Partner. That is something we would never do because it is out of alignment with our core value of complete Client-Partner dedication.

Throughout the process, we understand that your magazine is going to be an immediate representation of you and your brand, so it needs to be exactly how you want it.

Even when things don't go as planned, we never blame anybody or anything. We either succeed or we choose not to do it before we start. Once we've taken on a project, there's no going back for us, and we will overcome any obstacle to achieve that coveted final result.

We often have Client-Partners ask if we will sell the advertising for their magazine, which would require us to foster relationships with advertisers on their behalf. We do not do this because we know that we can't succeed at it. Our Client-Partners have the relationship with these advertisers; we don't. This makes them the best ones to reach out to those advertisers. We will dig in and assist to build a list of possible advertisers. But we are unable to sell the advertising and we know this, so we choose not to do it because we are not able to succeed at it.

Our Client-Partners have also asked us to manage their social media for them, which we have also humbly declined to do. Since we do not live and breathe in their organizations every day, we are not able to supply their unique tone and branding. The best fit to post on their social media is themselves. We could easily take over their posting, but we would not succeed at it 100 percent, so we choose not to do it. (We do, however, assist in creating content and graphics that they can post in conjunction with a written message.)

We fully understand that if you do not see success from the program, there is no point in pursuing it. We're going to make sure that you see that success. To us, building that success for you looks like generating leads, nurturing your clients, and thinking strategically to grow your business.

All of our programs are designed with these principles in mind. If we are not helping to make you—our Client-Partners—successful, then why are we in the picture?

Erika personally recalls one crazy night. She and Jessica had been taking shifts all night while they monitored the stats for a Client-Partner's book to reach Amazon Best-Seller status. When Andy arrived on the West Coast late at night (very early that morning on the East Coast) after a long flight, he decided to check the stats himself and chimed in with some encouraging words, not expecting a reply until morning. He was surprised to find both Jessica and Erika awake at 3:00 a.m. to chat back to him and let him know they were working hard to get the Client-Partner across the line for that best-seller goal. By morning, they had done just that!

There is so much more to what we do than simply creating a magazine or newsletter. This is especially true since the addition of SMarketing to our program offerings.

One of the things we took on during the COVID-19 crisis was a key role in communication efforts. We understood that our Client-Partners needed assistance with their communication immediately, so we developed a content library that was specifically based around COVID-19. We made it easy for them with a solid prewritten foundation article they could simply tailor to reflect their business tone and message.

We recognize how much easier it is to tweak an article and make it yours than it is to start from scratch. We created over twenty different articles that served as the basis of this communication.

Each article was unique. From content based around tips and tricks for working from home to helpful hints for leaders looking to downsize, there was a little something for everyone. It was stuff that could be pulled, tweaked, and sent out within hours.

There was so much going on that we just wanted to help out in any way we could.

Andy started doing daily two-minute videos in which he would give a different motivational survival tip each day of the pandemic. In addition to being the founder and CEO of Tulip Media, Andy is a successful certified Scaling Up business coach.

A lot of thought went into making these videos valuable for everyone who took that couple of minutes to tune in each day. It also brought some consistency to our Client-Partners' routines and reinforced that they were not alone in this; we were right in there with them. It really helped to build a sense of community throughout the pandemic and kept that teamwork mentality alive while everyone struggled with how to move forward.

We really do take the success of our Client-Partners to heart. We go above and beyond every day to see this through.

Throughout COVID, we became even more flexible with our working hours and what we were willing to do to help. Although some of our Client-Partners are located six time zones away, we made sure we were on standby to answer their calls when they needed us.

At first, many of our Client-Partners were working from sunup to sundown just trying to maneuver through this. We tried to be very respectful of their time. If we needed to do Zoom calls at six o'clock in the morning or nine o'clock at night, we didn't hesitate to do it. We didn't want to add any unnecessary or time-consuming communication tasks. Anything that did not help, we set aside. Our focus was 100 percent on getting them through.

We also take on a lot of small tasks behind the scenes that often go unseen. These are not necessarily related to the standard program offering; however, we know it's going to make life easier for our Client-Partner, so we take the initiative at no extra cost.

This initiative emerges in various forms for our diverse base of Client-

Partners. Sometimes it takes the form of researching products that might be of value to them; sometimes it means working with their website designers to flesh out branding and create consistency throughout publications. None of this is necessarily part of the magazine program, but it is something that we have some expertise in and knowledge to share. Our contribution to your overall marketing strategy extends far beyond your existing program.

A few years back we recreated a Client-Partner's magazine three times. There had been some miscommunication within their company and also some turnover within their marketing department. At one point during the design process, they'd even decided to change some of their branding guidelines.

We were also in the process of rebranding at the time, so we were very sympathetic to their situation. We had seen marketing do a full pivot halfway through the creation of their magazine, but we remained committed to creating the best product that matched their idea of what was needed for success.

Putting this much additional effort into a magazine would never be an expectation of us, but we care about your success as a company so greatly that we will go above and beyond to ensure your needs are met and that you are proud of the finished product. This applies even in a case such as this where dynamics are shifting within your own company, but we take the onus on us to make life easier for you.

A third point falling under our complete Client-Partner dedication is a promise that if it is within our means logistically, we will make it happen. Sometimes our Client-Partners will ask us to do something that, again, is not part of our normal process. Without saying "That's not what we do," we look into it instead. If we can figure out a way to make it happen— either by outsourcing something or using some of our connections in the industry—we will negotiate and we will make it happen.

We once had a Client-Partner say, "We need a magazine, but we need it next week because we have a trade show." Not to mention it was the week of Thanksgiving in the United States! Nonetheless, we knew we could afford to outsource some current work and set aside some less time-sensitive items, so we jumped right in to help. We got off the call on a Monday and had the magazine uploaded for print by Friday.

After publication, we made arrangements for the printed magazines to be delivered directly to their trade show booth right on time. This was something that we were all so proud of, to be able to get them what they needed in such a short time and over Thanksgiving, no less! If it is within our means logistically, one way or another, we will make it happen.

Finally, when we learn about an issue, we own the issue regardless of whose problem or project it is. When we find out that something has become an issue for a Client-Partner, we will 100 percent figure out a way to resolve it. Whether it is with our writers, printers, advertisers, or distributors, we take it upon ourselves to make things right.

Even if it's not our problem, we make it our problem so that it doesn't become your problem. We go above and beyond to make everything easy for our Client-Partners, and this is just one more example of this. In this case, we are in your corner and happy to work with advertisers and more on your behalf to get the situation resolved.

A few years ago, in our second year of business, we had an advertisement duplicated accidentally in one of our magazines. The magazine had already been printed 30,000 times and was ready for the post office when we discovered the error. When we went back, we realized there had been a mix-up with the upload that had gone to print. To make things right, we recreated the magazine and printed another 30,000 copies. This was all to ensure that, at the end of the day, our Client-Partner was happy.

Again, this was not necessarily our mistake, but we took it upon ourselves to make it right. We look back on it now as a $10,000 lesson that we learned, and we have put a few additional checkpoints in place to prevent it from happening again.

We take this stance whenever there is an issue. Instead of playing the blame game and using a reprimand strategy, we always figure out how it can help us in the future and how we can make sure it doesn't happen again. Because of this, we're always learning, adapting, and trying to come up with a better process and new ways of doing things. This attitude takes the onus off of our Client-Partners and keeps all of our systems refined and on point.

Above all, we are dedicated to standing behind our Client-Partners always and doing what it takes to see your successes through, no matter what. Complete and utter dedication to you is at the forefront of our core values for good reason, and we look forward to showing you just what this means every day we work together.

"In determining the right people, the good-to-great companies placed greater weight on character attributes than on specific educational background, practical skills, specialized knowledge, or work experience."

— Jim Collins, Business Consultant, Author of *Good To Great*

# Chapter Seven

## ACT AND THINK LIKE
## AN ENTREPRENEUR

*"You have to be odd to be #1." - Dr. Seuss*

---

"You have to be odd to be number one." This is something we remind ourselves of daily. We encourage each other to be odd and to think outside the box. Thinking like an entrepreneur means embracing those odd new ideas and running with them. We've uncovered some amazing new techniques for problem solving and revamped our internal systems and more this way.

Not only do we think like entrepreneurs but we also act like them, each one of us, day in and day out. This means we are dedicated, conscientious, and take responsibility for our own actions and results. We honor our commitments with pride and make it a priority to do what we say we are going to do, every time.

We are hungry for success both individually and as a team, and we will do what it takes to succeed. Because we think and act like entrepreneurs, we are mindful of what success means and what it looks like. Part of this mind-set is an acknowledgement that we cannot succeed at everything, so we understand how to differentiate and when to say no.

In action, we either pursue complete success at what we choose to do or we choose not to do it. It really is that simple, and we all understand the importance of this. We are not a company that accepts every project that comes our way because we appreciate that we may not be the best fit for every company. We know what we are good at, and we tailor our program offerings to capitalize on our refined skill sets.

Part of what makes our workplace culture so unique and wonderful is that all of us are empowered to act like owners. One of the processes we have in place is that any two people have the authority to make a decision if it is in the best interest of the company as a whole. It doesn't matter who those two people are, if any two of us can agree that a given change is in Team Tulip's best interest, we are empowered to make that change on behalf of the organization.

We never blame anything or anyone for mistakes, but we do overcome them together.

At Tulip Media, we are transparent about our financials. Each month, we gather as a team to review the previous month's profit and loss. Each quarter, we review the quarterly statements. It aids our collective mindset to know that each working member of the team is also a valued company stakeholder. This means all of us benefit when the company is doing well. Acting as both employees and stakeholders motivates us to be inherently mindful of spending and to consistently expand our comfort zone in the company interest.

Each member of the team reviews one or more line items on the profit and loss each month. This has enabled many of us to become actual stakeholders of the company. We've all taken the time to educate ourselves with an understanding of basic bookkeeping concepts, so we are more than capable of performing a thorough analysis of the details of each line item of the profit and loss. If there are any transactions we are not comfortable with, we bring them up at the team meeting for discussion. We believe everyone on our team should always be made aware of the company's financial position. At Tulip Media, all employees are given the option to buy shares into the company each year.

Another way we instill entrepreneurship throughout is putting the company sales responsibilities on the shoulders of our entire team. Instead of designating a select few people to focus on making sales, we are all responsible for making sales. This embodies our inbound sales model and is part of the SMarketing process that eliminated our need for a sales team.

Since we no longer have a sales team generating leads, we utilize several online platforms and our individual Calendly accounts. Calendly performs a "round robin" and splits the inbound sales calls out between us, making us each responsible for an equal percentage of leads. From there, we use individual Salesforce accounts to track the sales activities. Each morning, we update the team on the progress of leads that have come through our individual funnels. Every Monday, we review our active opportunities together to strategize on specific sales activities. This keeps us all accountable and holds each member of the team to a standard of follow up and turnaround time. It's in our best interest to close as many sales as possible and to work as a team to do this.

Even though we are each responsible for our own leads, we do not hesitate to seek out the expertise of another team member to convert an opportunity into a closed sale. At the end of the year, we all benefit from our "Great Game of Business" profit-sharing payout.

A few years ago, we had a stretch where several Client-Partners had opted out of our programs and we were all approached to take a temporary pay cut in order to keep the company afloat. Every member on the team agreed to take this pay cut and maintained it for six months. It's not often that a team together will take a pay cut, so it's fair to say we've all been effectively conditioned to think and act like entrepreneurs. Any of us could have looked for a new job at any time, but that wasn't even on anyone's mind. We all knew we wanted to be here, and we all knew we wanted this company to succeed. Taking a small hit for a short time was worth it.

We all have a commendable work ethic and take on a leadership role within the organization. The synergy we've created internally really fuels this because we are constantly motivated to work hard for continuous growth.

We tell our Client-Partners that we are open twenty-four hours, seven days a week. This might sound impossible in theory, but wait until you see it in action. By no means does this mean we are working at every second of every day. Each person on our team has a life and loved ones that remain a priority and hobbies to fill free time, but we do make sure we are available in case of an urgent matter or quick question at all hours of every day.

If Client-Partners contact us by email, it comes straight to our phone, and it is our goal to get back to them as quickly as possible. If our Client-Partners contact us by telephone, we will answer no matter where we are or what time of day. We could be away from our office and unable to answer their questions or concerns right then, but at the very least, we will reply to their email or answer that telephone call just to let them know we will get back to them with an answer as soon as we can.

It is important to our Client-Partners—who are located all over Canada and the United States, often in different time zones—that we maintain this around-the-clock regiment, and we are happy to do so because we value our partnerships with them. We respect that their jobs are equally as important as ours, and we prioritize our commitment to serve them. This small gesture has continually seen our Client-Partners rave about our customer service to others and created many opportunities for new client-partnerships.

As entrepreneurs at Tulip Media Group, we also have a very relaxed vacation policy. In fact, our allotted vacation time is limitless, and we are welcomed to take as much vacation as we like. Even though our vacation policy is unlimited, we act and think like entrepreneurs in that no one takes advantage of this. We all do enjoy it, but we make sure our work is done before we leave the office. On average, it often equates to less than standard vacation time because we all love our jobs so much that we don't often feel we need to get away from them.

In our absence, we do not leave things for others to pick up the slack, just as any business owner would know better than to do.

On our team, we have two types of "out of office." Our OOO setting means that we are out of office but that we are available if there is something urgent needed. We also have a PTO setting, which means we are taking personal time off and ask not to be bothered during this time. Everyone needs time away from work sometimes, and we can all appreciate this.

Knowing that we can trust each other to respect boundaries when it is needed plays a huge role in keeping our team energized to go the extra mile.

We had a Client-Partner approach us for a last-minute magazine around Christmas time one year. The magazine was needed for a conference coming up in early January. It was a tight timeline to begin with, but then we also had the Christmas holidays to deal with. On top of that, we usually take two full weeks off for Christmas break!

It was a large contract that we were all very excited to have, and we were all willing to do what it took to succeed at it. Needless to say, in order to have the magazine arrive at the trade show on time, there was no way we were going to be able to take that break. As a team, we worked through the Christmas holidays, got the magazine out in the mail, and delivered to the trade show in record time. This just goes to show that we really do have a tenacious work ethic and truly will do what it takes to succeed for our company and for our Client-Partners.

We think like entrepreneurs and take responsibility for our own actions and results. When we take projects like this on, we understand the implications for our own roles, and we decide individually and as a team what we are capable of and what we have the capacity for. Because our own values are aligned so well with the core values of the company, it's easy for us to synchronize our thinking and decide what is in the best interest of everyone, including ourselves, our Client-Partners, and the organization as a whole.

As we have all recently become salespeople within the organization, we now have the added responsibility of owning our results in this regard. We each have sales calls that come in at all hours of the day and night. If it is our lead or our opportunity, we are responsible for making ourselves available to answer those calls and for getting the information to those potential Client-Partners no matter the time of day. Our potential and existing Client-Partners are located across North America—primarily in the United States, in fact—so we need to work across several time zones to effectively accommodate those incoming requests.

Owning mistakes and taking responsibility for our actions is inherent in everything that we do. As dedicated members of Tulip Media Group, we are all tasked with resolving issues that arise in our line of duty. Sometimes this means asking for help, and sometimes it doesn't.

A number of years ago, we had an issue with a United States bank. There was an error where about $11,000 was taken from our business account and put into someone else's. When we noticed the funds had been taken from our account, we immediately contacted the bank. The bank had an issue with their ACH platform, which is comparable to the EFT platform in Canada. In effect, this $11,000 payment ended up going in the wrong direction.

Being the one in charge of our ACH payments, Stacey felt horrible about this and worked tirelessly with the bank to try to get it fixed. The result after weeks of phone calls and email correspondences with the bank was that there was nothing they could do. The other party had withdrawn the funds and closed their account knowing the funds did not belong to them. How does a United States bank today let an error like this happen? Stacey was beyond frustrated and could not imagine how a bank could make a mistake like this and not take any responsibility for the loss, especially when the loss was a result of a technical error that had nothing to do with us.

So, Stacey persisted. In her eyes, she had no choice but to do so because at that time, $11,000 was everything to us. It was our next payroll, and we needed to have it back. There was no way she could accept that it was just gone.

The bank tried to push her away, but she explained to them over and over again that we were not going to just walk away from funds our company was relying on. This had to be corrected, and soon. Relief was written all over her face the day the bank called to say that they would be covering these funds out of their own pocket. It was a bank error, after all.

Even though this mistake was not Stacey's, the bank accounts are her responsibility, and her obligation to maintain them is not something she takes lightly. As soon as she noticed the mistake, she took it upon herself to resolve the matter without putting the burden on anyone else. It was her line of duty, and she saw the resolution through to the end.

Another thing none of us takes lightly is our responsibility to honor our commitments. We make it a priority to do what we say we are going to do, every time. Sometimes this has meant losing a little sleep, but ultimately, we always follow through. If we don't think we can follow through on a project, we don't take the project on.

Above all, we are committed to thinking critically and seeking out the best approach and resolution for every situation. Our focus is never on knowing *what* to think but on learning *how* to think and acting on the results of that thinking in a way that produces the greatest benefit for everyone involved. This is part of what makes working with our entire team so refreshing and rewarding. We are truly dedicated to acting and thinking like entrepreneurs and encouraging everyone to be the best that they can be, always.

**"You can build a much more wonderful company on love than you can on fear."**

— Kip Tindell, CEO,
The Container Store

# Team Tulip

## PHOTOS

Andy Buyting.
CEO & Founder

Erika MacLeod,
Managing Editor / Publisher

Stacey O'Brien,
VP of Everything

Jessica Embree,
Creative Director

Celebrating our new water cooler.

Team Tulip staff numbers.

Our version of 'Elf on the Shelf' featuring Andy.

Office Renos!

Jessica's Wedding!

The whole company got "tattoos" to celebrate the rebrand!

# Chapter Eight

## RELENTLESS ABOUT QUALITY, EASE AND ROI

*"It's not about what it is, it's about what we can become." - Dr. Seuss*

---

At Tulip Media, we obsess about return on investment (ROI) for our Client-Partners and for ourselves. This belief is imbued in every single action we take. For us, it's not just about putting words to paper or words on a website or blog. We recognize that there is so much more to the process than this. Immense thought goes into writing a great piece of content or copy.

We always look first to what we want the article or message to do. Do we want this article to inform our readers? Is there a call to action at the end that invites the audience to call our Client-Partner or to purchase a featured product? We also look at keyword strategy and determine where we want to gain those SEO points for each piece.

For instance, there are a great many ways to go about creating an article. Sometimes Client-Partners don't realize how flexible the process can be while maintaining the highest professional standard. There are a number of very specific ways in which articles can be written, and we always adapt our processes to better accommodate our Client-Partners.

As part of our own process, we find it consistently effective to perform a keyword analysis with each Client-Partner. This helps us better understand what your goals are for search engine optimization and how we can make your articles perform their very best. We really want to hit those keywords you are competing for and leverage that to boost your rankings.

Adding value is of utmost importance to our team. When we say we are relentless about quality, we mean it. We work closely with all of our Client-Partners to produce engaging content that will be meaningful and valuable to their target audience. In fact, we've mastered the art of creating content that drives conversions, and we're eager to share our processes with you as we go on to build a mutually profitable partnership.

One of the other things that everyone here at Tulip Media is really digging into is the art of copywriting.

Donald Miller, CEO and founder of StoryBrand. To generate more leads for your business, Don has created a methodology that focuses on creating clear and impactful messaging that resonates with your customers.

We realized the importance of this StoryBrand methodology and, as a company, decided to become StoryBrand Agency Certified.

What started our journey with StoryBrand—and eventually led us to become StoryBrand Agency Certified—was the realization that we weren't being effective in our sales and marketing process. Back in 2019, we were making hundreds of cold calls every day and investing in trade show after trade show—and none of it was working. We were beyond frustrated because we knew our services could really help businesses grow and thrive. The problem was that we were focusing on our services and forgetting whom our core customer was. We were making Tulip Media the "hero" in the story, meaning we started off talking about ourselves in every communication that we did with potential Client-Partners. We realized that although the messaging we were using was important, it was not an impactful first impression. Enter StoryBrand.

After discovering the StoryBrand Framework, we proceeded to read all of Donald Miller's books and take all of his courses. We then took the leap in December 2020 to become StoryBrand Agency Certified. Although our SMarketing program had already been rolled out at this time, we knew going the extra mile to get our certification would add more value to the programs we were already providing to our Client-Partners.

There are only about 32 StoryBrand Certified Agencies in the world, so in that respect, you may consider us a rare breed, especially since we are just the second company in all of Canada to get this certification.

Our second target in producing a palpable return on investment is to make the entire process effortless for our Client-Partners. We want our working systems to be so seamless and easy to use that you can't help but buy from us. From start to finish, we will adapt, always enlisting the means to make you comfortable and stress free in the commanding role for every project. This often looks different for each Client-Partner, and we are happy to accommodate. Everything we do is centered around making your life easier and improving the flow of business through engaging content both digitally and in print.

Our content library gives our Client-Partners access to hundreds of articles and the ability to choose articles that resonate with their brand. They can then publish the articles directly as is or tweak the article to make it their own. At the very least, it's a perfect starting point for curating great content that is sure to engage readers.

If our Client-Partners are not sure what they want published in their magazines, we will make recommendations. This might mean doing some research into the sorts of things we've seen in similar magazines. We often pass around some ideas that we have seen others do where the results were spectacular. We are always looking to help, and we'll only make suggestions we truly believe will add value for our Client-Partners. Ultimately, we want each magazine to be as beautiful as it can be and to look professional. Whatever we can do to make that happen more efficiently is a bonus for us and our Client-Partners.

Our team of designers is always up to date with the latest in design trends and new ways of doing things. They are all masters of creating eye-catching images and making the overall finished product look visually appealing.

We want to be the ones who do all of the design and aesthetics research for you. Staying current and furthering our education internally is a major priority for keeping our services optimized, and this translates directly into our aptitude for quality work. Again, we do all of the heavy lifting so you can sit back and keep your focus where it is needed most— on your business.

Another way that we achieve far-reaching results is through the use of talented ghostwriters. Oftentimes it can be difficult to just sit down and write 1,000 words on a specific topic, even if it's your area of expertise. Sometimes, you just don't have the time.

Our job is to arrange an interview with you and a writer we feel is compatible with your needs. Each of our ghostwriters goes through an interview and assessment process similar to those of our staff, so you can rest assured they know their stuff.

All of our ghostwriters are accustomed to the ghostwriting process and operate under the expectation their work will be published under a different name. That's their job, and they take great pride in transforming your ideas into a professional article or blog post that you can gladly display as your own.

The ghostwriter will give you a call for the first time when it's convenient for both of you to talk. They'll speak with you for around twenty minutes about what you're looking for and how they can help. Following the interview, they will create the article for you and send it over for review and editing. You'll agree that it is much easier to edit an existing article than to start from scratch.

If you prefer a written interview format, we're okay with that too! Just go ahead and put down ten points in an email that you'd like covered in the article. We'll return a fully researched article for you to review. We're also happy to provide you with several shorter 500-word sample articles if you'd like to get a feel for which writing style works best for you. The goal of this process is to get your knowledge written down for your audience to consume in the most efficient and resonant way possible.

Whether you're using the articles for your magazine or website, it's important to us that the final product looks professional and stands out no matter what. Blog posts should be illuminated with eye-catching images, and your magazine should be able to hold its own on the shelf with many other magazines. That's what we're here to achieve for you.

We never accept second best for our Client-Partners. We always make a point of exceeding performance expectations and delivering the absolute best.

We have some amazing designers on our team that use a range of tools to accommodate design needs. For example, if the quality of imagery is low, we can sometimes reproduce it as high-resolution with one of our software solutions. We have gone to great lengths to recreate images that weren't quite sharp enough for print. This isn't something that would generally be expected of a design team, but it just goes to show how we will consistently go the extra mile to deliver tremendous quality of service and product.

Another way we meet our exceptional performance standards is by digging deep into our distribution research. If there is a locale that a Client-Partner wants their magazine to be distributed to, we will find out who in that neighborhood would be interested in purchasing their products and services. Then we'll work with the Client-Partner to decide how to approach that market.

If we really don't think you can benefit from distribution to a certain area, we'll let you know.

We do not guess when it comes to what our Client-Partners want nor do we assume. Too often we see the "no news is good news" mentality in action, but that is not the case at Tulip Media. When we are in doubt or haven't heard back, we will reach out to you to make sure everything is OK and to see if there is anything further we can offer to help.

Checking in to make sure everything is going okay is built into our processes, especially while we are in production. We all take it upon ourselves to have everything covered, and each of us takes responsibility for this when the project is in our line of duty.

We also take responsibility as a whole during daily team huddles and one-on-one meetings.

If a few days have passed in silence, that's when we step up and speak up because sometimes a Client-Partner has hit a roadblock, but they are so busy, they just don't have time to say, "Hey, I need some help here." By checking in, we avoid dragging this process out to the point where it becomes inconvenient. As soon as we sense something might not be running entirely as planned, we want to jump in and rectify the situation. We believe this is an effective approach and ultimately the right one when it comes to managing our client-partnerships.

We always do the right thing for our clients, our team, and our shareholders. If our team is one thing, it's extremely cost-conscious. This point is really reflected in the way we operate. We are always thinking about how we can negotiate a better deal on paper costs, distribution, etc. We always review costs with the team and discuss ways that we can do better next month, quarter, or year. All of us take these figures very seriously and try to think outside the box when it comes to driving them down. Fundamentally, we are always working on a more efficient and cost-effective way of doing things.

Each year we go over everything in our office, from printers to paper. This is the real wake-up call.

We price out what we paid and what we are paying versus the price tag of available alternatives. Now that we are all working from home, our tolerance for office expenses has been slashed again because we only require a fraction of the resources. We have, however, invested in some quality digital collaboration software.

After COVID hit, we noticed that our entire team was able to bounce back almost immediately. Within a couple of hours of everyone dispersing from our physical office, all of us were already up and running again from home. This was due in part to the freedom we'd previously had to work from home two days a week. It also said a lot about the return on investment we required of our hardware and software and the attention we paid to costs. It demonstrated that we were effective in maximizing our use of the minimum required to be successful in our roles.

Not only did this save us money in the long term but it saved us invaluable time when we were able to painlessly move into the work-from-home environment using only the essentials.

Although we've now eliminated the physical office space entirely, we have reserved a much smaller space for a once-a-week, face-to-face team meeting for those who live in our hometown. As social beings (especially Erika and Jessica), we acknowledge the importance of maintaining that physical connection even though we are all working from home.

Nonetheless, we remain conscious of everything coming in and going out, and we constantly obsess over the most efficient use of our resources. Nobody gets by spending frivolously or jumping to buy something that might not be worth its price tag or available for a lower price somewhere else. We always get a second quote and refine our buying processes to better maintain our financial stability.

Because most employed by Tulip Media are also partners, we all have our heart and soul invested in its success. We also have that financial piece on each of our shoulders that keeps us individually conscientious of the company funds we spend. I think this is one of the best ways to make employees act like owners, because we are, and our actions reflect that we really do own a little piece of this.

From what we buy to what we give, this core value stands strong and reflects the mind-set that has seen us through COVID and continuing down the path to rapid growth. We are proud to be relentless.

"Presenting leadership as a list of carefully defined qualities (like strategic, analytical, and performance-oriented) no longer holds. Instead, true leadership stems from individuality that is honestly and sometimes imperfectly expressed . . . Leaders should strive for authenticity over perfection."

— Sheryl Sandberg, COO Of Facebook
And Founder Of LeanIn.org

# Chapter Nine

## LEADERSHIP, TEAMWORK
## AND OPEN COMMUNICATION
*"Open your mouth lad for every voice counts." - Dr. Seuss*

---

One of the great ways that we communicate at Tulip Media is through our daily huddles. Every morning at 8:47 a.m. we come together to discuss how the day is going to unfold and more. We used to do these huddles around the office when we were all in the office. Now we do them via Zoom.

There's a reason we choose to have our huddles at 8:47 a.m. versus a standard time like a quarter to nine. The reason being is that when you choose a standard time, you end up having people show up a few minutes early or a few minutes late. This can create a lack of clarity and awkwardness settling everyone down when it's time to start. When you choose an odd time like 8:47 a.m., there is no ambiguity about when the actual meeting starts, and there is no implied expectation to be early because the specificity indicates that we  are expected to start at exactly 8:47 a.m. This really eliminates any wasted time.

We have a set agenda that we follow. We talk about our biggest win from the day before, go over what's on each person's plate for today, and any "stucks" we might have. It really pushes us to be transparent about what we accomplished yesterday and what's going on today. Often one person's "stuck" can be handled very easily by someone else in the group, which maintains the pace of our workflow.

Daily huddles keep us accountable and on track, but it's also nice to be informed about what everyone else is doing. This keeps us in the loop and motivated to maintain a comparable work ethic. Since each person is their own piece of the puzzle, per se, understanding where they are in a given project helps each of us be better prepared when it's time to hand that project off to the next person.

We used Slack when we were working in the office to quickly transfer files or send a quick message across the room. We use email only for specific task items that are meant to remain in our inboxes until completed. All other internal communication is done via Slack. It's a quicker, easier means of asking those little back-and-forth questions rather than dedicating an entire email thread to them. Now that we all work from home, we are on Slack constantly. We like to say now that when you need us, we're all "just a quick Slack away."

For "face-to-face" meetings, Zoom allows us to connect with team members and potential and existing Client-Partners. We can confidently use Zoom for all our daily huddles and meetings with Client-Partners without concern that the call will be interrupted or dropped.

Our favorite weekly get together is Beer O'Clock, which is the hour between 4 o'clock and 5 o'clock on Fridays. We all pour ourselves a drink, whether it be beer or wine, at home. We used to have wine and beer on standby in the office fridge; now we all joke that we have to buy our own. Having a scheduled time to relax together on the clock is a fun way to debrief on the week and hear about each other's plans for the weekend. It also helps us get to know each other better.

Our team is so much more than just workmates. We're all friends outside the office too. Sometimes we go to the same hangout spots and events. Maybe we're doing the same activity around our community or we just want to meet up at the market. Our workplace culture really fosters these relationships, and in turn, these relationships really foster our strong workplace culture.

We also do one-on-ones with Andy every week. In that half an hour, we have Andy's undivided attention. We talk about what happened last week, what we've got going on this week, if there are any problems he needs to be aware of or "stucks" that he needs to resolve. It's extremely helpful and comforting to know we can count on having that thirty minutes each week despite Andy's crazy busy schedule and our own.

Another example of how open communication plays a key role here at Tulip Media is our annual review process. Once a year, Andy will review our performance and provide challenges that he feels suit our personalities. This goes back to creating culture around DNA, not resume. He'll let us know what challenges he feels would be appropriate for us to tackle based on our skill set, with little regard for our formal job description. He loves to challenge us based on who we are and grow us in ways that help us blossom as people first and employees second.

One time, while Stacey was in her performance review, we packed her entire desk up into three boxes and joked that we thought she was in there getting fired. Obviously, we knew that wasn't true, but we wanted to play into her distaste for her review. When she came out of the meeting, her desk was all packed up with a pink slip sticking out from underneath the boxes. She laughed and then we laughed at the effort it had taken to remain quiet for thirty minutes while we packed up her desk. It's the little things like this that we miss in our virtual office setting. Pulling that off from our home offices while she was in a one-on-one via Zoom just wouldn't be logistically feasible.

A unique aspect of our annual review process is that we get to do a 360-degree review with Andy in the hot seat. It's unfortunate that more CEOs don't practice this, but we really respect Andy's passion for learning and growing himself, too, along with us. This plays a huge role in the culture we've developed. The best part is that Andy really appreciates feedback and constructive criticism. He doesn't want us to just sit back, nod, and say everything's great. He really wants to understand where he could improve and grow, and what he could work on. He's very open to constructive criticism and creates a space where we are comfortable to speak up and give feedback, not just to him but to everyone in our office. Of course, we do this respectfully and with candor.

There are some ways that we give feedback jokingly. For example, Erika has a habit of getting excited and interrupting people when she thinks of a story and wants to jump in. This is just part of her chatty nature and no one holds it against her, but we did come up with a fun way to combat it without making her feel bad. Now when she interrupts, anyone in the office can very kindly say "hummus!" to remind her to speak in turn. It's actually evolved into a bit of a standing joke to the point where Stacey's Slack notification sound says "hummus!" instead of dinging.

We use fun tools like this to communicate more effectively and to create an environment that manages our sticky habits without making anyone feel ashamed or unwanted because of those habits.

One of the other things we do is what we call a sales sprint. In the morning, if we have a sales challenge with a potential Client-Partner or an existing Client-Partner that we'd like to approach from a new angle, we can schedule a 15-minute meeting where everyone throws out ideas on how to handle the situation effectively. Because we all come at the problem from a different angle, there is a lot of ground covered in those fifteen minutes beyond what we could accomplish standing alone and so close to the problem. It is a highly effective way to tackle any problem and typically ends with amazing results.

Another thing we communicate effectively as a team is our financials. We are all expected to review statements and raise any concerns in our monthly financial review meetings. Because many of us are actually stakeholders of Tulip Media ourselves, it's important for us to be involved in the financial assessment of our company and especially planning for growth. We know where every penny of our money goes.

When we gather, each month we look at the revenues we brought in and the expenses we laid out. Once a quarter, we review our quarterly results to determine where we landed in terms of sales, expenditures, and profits so we can compare them against our targets. Ultimately, we recognize that we can't help the company save money when we don't know what our financial position is to begin with. Sometimes we're hit with the realization that a certain project cost way more than we expected, so we put our heads together on ways we can improve our cost-benefit results next time by being more financially responsible.

For each project, we allot projected revenues and expenses in advance, so there isn't a whole lot of communication required during the project to stay on track. We all have access to the budget for any given project. What's important is where we land at the end of the month and at the end of the quarter. All of the financials are completely open to everybody at any time.

Having access to financials is very empowering and also comes with great responsibility. We have a high level of dedication that is required to perform well in our respective roles, and a commitment to being educated enough to assess financial reports in a meaningful way is important to the growth of the company as a whole. We also need to have a "can-do" attitude when handling financial issues, like the example of Stacey and the bank that made a $11,000 mistake, and other tasks that arise. This is paramount to our success as a company and as a team.

An example of this "can-do" attitude in action is actually the process of writing this book. Out of a quarterly planning session very early in April—as COVID-19 was hitting and we were entering lockdown—one of our shareholders suggested that now would be the perfect time for us to write a book. At first, we were a bit shocked, but the more we thought about it, the more excited we got. It didn't take long for us to get fully on board and jump right in and do it.

We joke in the office about one of Andy's sayings: he's always telling us to jump out of the plane and build the parachute on the way down. We often know we'll have to figure a project out as we go, but we don't let that scare us away from jumping. We have a work environment where we are all comfortable asking for help, and we know that we have all of the help we need available on the other end of the Slack chat. Knowing we have each other's backs really fuels the "can-do" positive attitude for all of us and encourages us all to go a step beyond our comfort zone.

Practicing this mind-set does not mean being naive or unrealistic in any sense. It just means that we are committed to doing what it takes to get the job done and to do it well.

Our attitudes and strong trust in each other have also enabled us to pivot quickly when the need arises. Previously, we had an amazing office culture where we got to see each other every day. Fortunately, we've been able to translate that online. We all still have our jokes and those little quirks that make each other smile.

One thing we really believe in is the "your success is my success" mentality, which shines through in our Client-Partner relationships and within our team. We are humble and always put the best interests of the team and the company before our own interests. We are a team, so it doesn't matter if I'm having an issue or you're having an issue; regardless, we are going to work together to resolve it because your success is my success and therefore your success is paramount.

One time, at around 5:30 in the evening, Erika and Jessica were just leaving the office when out of the blue they got a crazy call from some members of our team who were at a trade show outside the province. The box containing all of their handouts hadn't arrived, and they'd just received a message that the shipment had been damaged and was not going to arrive at all.

Prior to this, everyone else had gone down to the trade show a day early to prepare. Jessica and Erika were the only ones who had stayed behind to staff the office. The two had plans that evening, but that didn't stop them from turning on their heels in the parking lot and heading back into the office to handle the situation. Together, they assembled a box of makeshift materials for handing out at the trade show and dropped the box off at FedEx for overnight delivery. The two followed up with the shipment incessantly. Erika was on the phone with another delivery company at 9:30 at night directing them to the back door of a FedEx location where a FedEx employee she'd just spoken with was standing and waiting to receive it.

The next day, Erika had someone lined up at the hotel with a cart ready to receive the heavy package and deliver it directly to the trade show booth where Andy and the team were waiting. She was determined to make it happen, so she did. The package arrived about fifteen minutes before the trade show was scheduled to open.

The next day, Erika recalls looking at Jessica and smiling, unbelievably proud they had been able to drop everything and pull that off. It was pretty cool.

You can see that we take our jobs very seriously, but ourselves? Not so much. Our culture is very much defined by our lighthearted nature and our creative ways of making everyone feel comfortable and appreciated.

In the office, we love to eat. We joke to anyone coming into the office that there are two rules: you are not allowed to judge the portion size of what we eat, nor are you allowed to judge what we are eating at a certain time of day. We may be eating brownies at nine in the morning or we may be eating breakfast sandwiches at 4:30 in the afternoon.

We all used to bring food into the office because we had our own kitchen. The kitchen was always stocked with bagels and cream cheese along with other snacks if we got hungry during the work day. We even had a little breakfast program at work to make mornings and the commute a little smoother for all of us.

A few years ago, we had an office-wide Biggest Loser contest. At that time, it was three males against three females, and it was ridiculous. After two months, the total weight lost was in the negatives. The boys lost a total of six pounds, but the ladies somehow gained nine. We were supposed to put money on the line, but the boys never made us pay because they knew better than to rub it in, especially when we'd been trying really hard. The moral of the story quickly became that the women who carry a little extra weight live longer than the men who mention it.

For our quarterly sales goals, we always do some sort of fun theme and activity to go along with it. We've hidden playing cards all around the office and then gathered hands to play blackjack and other game-type things. We all have the book *The Little Engine That Could* on our desks because that was a theme one quarter. We've also had a spa day as a reward. These activities are typically silly and fun and are always team building in nature. We always do some sort of celebration to commemorate reaching and exceeding our goals.

"Connect the dots between individual roles and the goals of the organization. When people see that connection, they get a lot of energy out of work. They feel the importance, dignity and meaning in their job."

— Ken Blanchard and Spencer Johnson, Coauthors of *The One Minute Manager*

# Chapter Ten

## EMBRACING AND DRIVING CHANGE

*"Why fit in when you were born to stand out!" - Dr. Seuss*

At Tulip, we truly believe that the sky's the limit. We strive to always ask "Why not?" instead of "Why?" Always learning and constantly growing is what we do best.

We are continuously advancing ourselves. Our knowledge and skills are what we use to build Tulip Media Group, so we take our knowledge and education very seriously.

We make a point of never being satisfied when it comes to what we know. We are actively seeking opportunities for improvement. We all know that we were born to stand out, so we embrace and drive change within ourselves and our company every day.

To better understand this value, allow us to share our "2020 Painted Picture" with you, which Andy wrote in 2017. This year marked a real turning point for Tulip Media Group as we're sure it did for many other companies. For us, 2020 reinforced the significance of being aligned with our powerful set of core values, especially our aptitude for being changemakers.

The best way to ensure a prosperous future together is to take ownership of our actions and write the script for success ourselves. At Tulip Media, we start with a clear picture of what we want our future to look like, and then we work together to build a path to making it happen.

Our painted picture for 2020 outlines what we look like, how we act, and how we feel on December 31, 2020. Then we consistently create building blocks for getting there. Often, these building blocks require us to move outside of our comfort zone to explore new ideas. In 2020 more than ever, we've been pushed to do this, but together we are forging the path to get to where we want to be.

Reaching our goals on December 31, 2020, will be a time to celebrate. On January 10, 2021, we will gather to celebrate with every single employee and partner of Tulip Media along with members of our families. We are celebrating our success story as a growing Atlantic Canadian company that is beating the odds, competing internationally against multi-million dollar publishing firms across North America from our small city of Fredericton, New Brunswick.

> *The best way to ensure a successful future together is to take ownership and script it ourselves. At Tulip Media we start with a clear painted picture of what our future looks like and then work together to make it happen. Our painted picture outlines what we look, act and feel like on December 31, 2020.*

> *It's a Time to Celebrate! On January 10th, 2021, we gather to celebrate with every single employee and partner of Tulip Media along with members of our families. We are celebrating our success story as a growing Atlantic Canadian company that is beating the odds and competing internationally from our small town in Fredericton, New Brunswick. As I read through our 2018 Painted Picture, I am grateful to everyone who has had a hand in getting us where we are today.*

> **WE DID IT!**
> *In 2020, we accomplished a milestone that fewer than 3% of companies ever achieve, a company-wide revenue run rate of $3M! In doing so, we helped over 50 Client-Partners achieve greater business results. Overcoming challenges and succeeding together is a wonderful feeling.*

> **OUR CORE**
> *To empower others so they can achieve greater business results through easy and effective marketing strategies is what drives us*

*each day and is at the heart of everything we do. We are completely dedicated to their success, creating and distributing digital & print strategies that drive measurable results & outcomes.*

*As a team, we are guided by our five Core Values of Complete Client-Partner Dedication, Act & Think Like Entrepreneurs, Relentless About Quality, Ease and ROI, Leadership, Teamwork & Open Communication and Embrace & Drive Change. These core values that guide our actions each day are also what defines our company's brand to the outside world. We are proud of what our brand represents as they are directly tied to who we are and our values.*

### ENGAGEMENT & LEARNING

*Our people are engaged – switched on! With our focus on continuous learning, we grow our people, both professionally and personally. In fact, over the past couple of years, we have grown our people more than ever before – turning everyone into lead generating, content marketing ninjas for our Client-Partners! Our team is results driven, only retaining high performers  - Smart adults who get shit done!*

*By leveraging technology and lean in our work, we have become more efficient than most in our industry. As a high-performing team, we have accomplished a Gross Margin / Full Time Equivalent metric that is 3x larger than most marketing firms. Because of this, we are able pay top dollar for talent, and our people enjoy the satisfaction of being part of a successful company and the financial benefits that come from it.*

### LEADERSHIP

*Tulip Media is becoming an emerging leader in the marketing industry. Because of our success and our high-performing team, Tulip Media is on track to qualify for Canada's Growth 500 list of fastest growing companies in 2021.*

### CLIENT-PARTNER SERVICES

*Our programs and service offerings have evolved as we've transitioned to become trusted advisors and outsourced marketing partners for those we work with. Our team creates and delivers the right mix of digital, print & interactive marketing that drives results & measurable outcomes for our Client-Partners.*

*Leveraging the three pillars of effective marketing and executing with excellence, we have become an integral partner in our clients' success. In fact, they regularly note that a part of their growth is attributed to the work we do for them.*

### GROWTH
*We've successfully developed an effective marketing & sales strategy that produces results. Most of our sales start as inbound opportunities originating from our own digital, print and interactive marketing efforts. Our monthly ambassador revenue share payments are higher than ever, which means that our target audience knows who we are and are coming to us! As a result, our cost of acquisition has plunged to under $3,000 per new client!*

### SERVICE
*We are proud of the level of personalized service we provide our Client-Partners. We see every interaction as an opportunity to connect with them – from our welcome kit to our orientation session, from our weekly Client-Partner recognition process to our "Giftology" program, our entire team continuously looks for opportunities to "WOW" them!*

*We deliver what we promise. We're committed to our Brand Promises of Easy & Effective. Our Client-Partners know we've built something special. They take pride in the work we do for them and are reassured to know that they can count on us to deliver every time. They love it when they see the flurry of activity online and in their marketing efforts, knowing that Tulip Media is making a difference in their business.*

### SUCCESS!
*If there is one metric that we are most proud of, it's our exceptional Net Promoter Score, now a whopping 85%! Along with over 30 Google reviews collected, it's clear that our Client-Partners love Tulip Media!*

*Staying committed to a strategy of Effective Marketing Delivered – Easy. is what drives our profitability and success.*

*We grow the top line without ever taking our eyes off the bottom line. Standing here today, we are proud to announce our second year of profitability, with 2020 achieving a bottom line over $240,000! As such, we have paid off all operating debts and are looking forward to our Great Game of Business profit sharing coming soon!*

*Success means winning, contributing, being recognized and having fun. We work as a team to paint this picture of a respected and admired brand among the business communities we operate in. We support one another in reaching personal goals and we celebrate each milestone along the journey of making Tulip Media exceptional.*

During each quarterly planning session, we reread this painted picture as a group. To stay focused on what we want Tulip Media's future to look like, we start each quarter reading through our three-year goals together. We are fortunate that Andy is also a Certified Scaling Up Business Coach. We go through our quarterly planning sessions like clockwork, and they are efficient.

After we review our painted picture, we talk about the books that we've read over the last quarter and share what we've learned with the team. We then review our personal and company victories from the past three months, review our core values and how we've applied them, and then we jump into our financials for the previous quarter and review them as a team. We look at our one-year goals, priorities, and results, and finalize our meeting by updating our team dashboard with upcoming individual and company priorities for the next quarter. We always have a fun theme for our quarter. If we hit our goals or exceed them, we treat ourselves to a victory prize. In each weekly tactical meeting, we update the team on our progress toward achieving our goals.

There have been many changes to our product offerings since the early days of Tulip Media when we sold our magazines at cost and pushed profits through national advertising. The programs that we offer today have evolved tremendously. We've achieved this through constantly driving change into action. Believing the sky's the limit is what has brought all of this to fruition for us.

There were times throughout the years when the company was upside down and it made no sense for us to continue. Regardless, every person on the team believed that we could fully conquer the world. We had unwavering faith that we were going to be hugely successful even when rational people would have been worried about lasting for even another month.

We've used education to empower our team and to drive the changes necessary to our survival. A great way to get employees learning is to have them read. We subscribe to an online program called the BetterBookClub. This program is centered around rewarding employees for reading books. We each receive monetary compensation up to $100 a quarter for reading business-related books in our spare time. This has been an invaluable source of knowledge for everyone as we are all welcomed to share what we've learned with the team during weekly tactical and quarterly strategy meetings.

Remember that StoryBrand Agency Certification we mentioned earlier? As a company, we understood the value of the StoryBrand Framework and invested $40,000 to further our education with this methodology so we could extend this knowledge to our Client-Partners. We believe wholeheartedly that this Framework will help our Client-Partners get more leads. We have already seen such success.

Jessica took the plunge in December 2020 to be our Certified Guide at our company. Having a StoryBrand Certified Guide on the team also allowed all of us as a company to go through the training and become Agency Certified. The best part? Not only has everyone on our team upgraded their knowledge in marketing but we've already made back our $40,000 investment.

Each Monday afternoon, our team gathers for our weekly 'Grow Smart' meeting. During our Grow Smart meeting, we complete one hour of learning as a team. This learning can be anything from lengthy YouTube videos to webinars. We try to make learning relevant to what we are currently working on. Grow Smart, along with the BetterBookClub and our quarterly readings, is what keeps our team educated and up to date with the latest marketing methods and trends.

To work at Tulip Media means that you are constantly learning. In an average quarter, each employee reads over four books and takes part in almost eighteen hours of webinars. In addition, Tulip Media employees frequently go to world-class learning conferences where others pay several thousands of dollars to attend. One of these conferences is the Scale Up Summit. We've had numerous employees over the last several years that have jumped on the opportunity to attend this exemplary learning experience.

Along with our education, we build learning opportunities into the work that we do. The writing of this book is an excellent example. When we were first approached by Andy and Heidi to coauthor this book, Stacey did not think it would be possible for her to write a book, but it wasn't long before she found herself brimming with engaging content to fill the pages. Over several weeks, she was continuously adding stories throughout the book and turned this rare opportunity into a tremendous learning experience.

From letting our sales team go to shifting our entire marketing program almost overnight, embracing and driving change is a value we keep near and dear to the heart of Tulip Media. We look forward to what's to come as we continue to build ideas, drive change, and ultimately, grow in positive and exciting new ways.

"Always treat your employees exactly as you want them to treat your best customers."

— Stephen R. Covey, Author,
*The 7 Habits Of Highly Effective People*

# Chapter Eleven

## A LOOK BEHIND THE CURTAIN

---

Our team works tirelessly behind the scenes to make our Client-Partners proud. We work so seamlessly with you, your staff, and even your clients that it's hard to know just how much goes into providing the standard of service that you depend on.

One way of understanding what makes a good culture is understanding how our culture translates into building a strong brand. We have been fortunate to have achieved total cohesion over the years, and we work to nurture cohesiveness with our core values every single day.

Inside the company, we all know too well the different stages of production a magazine. Erika knows that she handles the overall organization of the project and the editing process, Heather handles design, Stacey handles distribution and accounting, and Jessica handles marketing. All of us fully understand our roles and what they entail. To someone on the outside, if they look behind the curtain, it may seem confusing because responsibility moves so quickly back and forth between stages, but each person on the team actually holds a very distinct piece of the puzzle. This is something that we are immersed in every day and that we are good at.

Working this way also holds us completely accountable. We know that if we are late getting started on our piece, we are going to put the next person behind, which is unfair to the entire team and something that we work relentlessly to avoid.

Inevitably, there are occasionally going to be hiccups, but we are masters at resolving them. We communicate with each other with respect and candor to get them resolved as quickly as possible. We always keep each other in the loop to avoid these issues whenever possible and to collaborate on solutions when we do hit a bump in the road.

If a certain task is taking longer than it should, someone else will usually pick up another small piece of the puzzle to help move the process along. Even though it's not our individual responsibility to pick up slack, all of us have a little bit of overlap in our positions, and that gives us the wiggle room to shuffle tasks back and forth as needed.

The communication piece is key to staying connected at all times. Our Slack channels are always open and ready to instantly respond to any incoming questions and issues as they arise. In our virtual world, constant communication like this is critical.

Tulip Media looks quite different these days than it did for those first few years. All of us are working from home offices and plan to keep it that way for the foreseeable future. This has meant a few minor changes to internal operations to keep us in total alignment with each other and the heart of our organization.

When Andy was sourcing furniture and equipment for our home offices, it was important to him that we all have a say in what we got. All of us know our positions better than anyone, so naturally we would each know our individual needs best. Andy actively acknowledged that our home offices were not to be a one-size-fits-all and that each should be adapted to our unique location, traits, and position within the company. Respect is intrinsic to the core values that make up Tulip Media, and the process of moving everyone home for good really spoke to Andy's character in this regard.

Some of us are farther along than others at outfitting our home offices. We've purchased all of the needed equipment for everyone to be effective. We've also ordered quite a few things online that we know will be necessary in the near future. It's essential that everyone's home office reflects what they need for their particular role.

Some of us have brought in massive three-section desks with large shelves on them; some have more modest desks that pivot on a dime. Each one of us needs something different for the way we work with the space we have available.

For Erika's office space, located in the corner of her dining room, she was able to find a pivoting desk online. It's able to open up when she needs it to and tucks away when she has family and friends over. It's also the perfect size to accommodate her two monitor screens and right handedness.

She actually jokes with Andy about the painful process of finding her perfect desk. Initially, the desk she was using was too small to accommodate all of her equipment. Then, she overestimated the amount of space she had and ended up receiving a massive desk that wouldn't even fit through her front door. Finally, she stumbled upon the pivoting desk online that was the perfect fit. The pivoting desk was a little on the expensive side, so Erika teased that if she couldn't make it work from home, she would need to join Andy in his home office where he would be the sole target in her line of sound. He purchased the desk for her that day.

Jessica has her office in the downstairs TV room of her family home. Stacey, Heather, Dorcas, and Andy all have extra rooms in their houses that have been converted into full-blown office spaces. They've also utilized large desks with lots of storage room. The point is that we always find a way to make it work!

We have done a lot of research into the various things we have brought into our home office spaces, such as printers, webcams, and lights. We really want to make sure we've got the right tools.

We always read the reviews to make sure we are getting something we really want and something that won't be surprisingly costly to maintain. For instance, we'll research the toner costs of any potential printer to forecast what the ongoing costs of that printer are going to be beyond that initial price tag. We are very cautious and careful to choose our products wisely.

Going further, we have created custom backgrounds for all of our Zoom calls. Each background has a custom arrangement of props with our logo prominently displayed in some regard. We are committed to doing it right, investing in technology and seeking out the right tools for the job. Our home offices should be reminiscent of our commitment to quality and our complete care for the work we do.

Operations are more efficient now than they have ever been. Nobody has to commute anymore, so we can focus on some of the things we are working on during this time instead. There are fewer distractions for our team while working from home, so if we want to spend two or three hours really digging deep into a project or just working away, it's easier to do that with minimal disruption. Sometimes an open office doesn't allow this because there is nothing stopping anyone from coming in and talking to you at any time.

We noticed right away how quickly and easily we were able to adapt to working in a virtual office full time. It really didn't cause so much as a hiccup in our work or day-to-day processes.

Additionally, we realized that not only would going virtual be more cost effective for us but it would also enable us to better serve our Client-Partners around the clock.

A huge part of what we do is take calls and fulfill requests at all hours of the day. Because our Client-Partners are located in different time zones across Canada and the United States, from the East Coast all the way to Hawaii, this is an essential part of our business model.

Being in the Atlantic time zone ourselves, it requires true dedication to ensure someone is available to take calls from our Client-Partners up to six hours behind our time zone. Regardless of where we are, making our service as efficient as possible for the time zone that you are in is always a priority for us.

Working virtually enables us to accommodate more rapid future growth. The talent pool we can tap into just got a whole lot larger as well. Whereas before we were limited to hiring in our small town area, working virtually gives us access to an unlimited number of qualified candidates outside our city. This is something we're really looking forward to exploring as time goes on, whether we seek talent across the continent or across the world.

Although we didn't need to add any new digital tools when we made the switch, we did change the way we used some online platforms. We started using Teamwork to make collaborative task lists. When help with a project was needed, it became easy and convenient to simply add a task to our colleague's working to-do list.

Abiding by our core values, we are always embracing change and striving to be better. Whenever we are introduced to a software that will work better for us, we are quick to research and jump on.

We are all fully capable of learning new software at any time, so staying with something relatively inefficient simply because we "already know it" is never a valid excuse on our team.

Something else we are focusing on now is refining the sales process and integrating the entire team into various sales activities. This means incorporating even more learning into our new normal.

We were already encouraged to take advantage of the company reading program in which we are paid to read books outside of working hours. Now, we are being further encouraged to take advantage of webinars and audio books. If a speaker sounds interesting, we all know the company will support us to join in and bring that material back into our work. If it not what we thought, there's no shame in just logging off or finding something else that speaks to the topic we were looking to explore.

**"Shaping your culture is more than half done when you hire your team."**

— Jessica Herrin, Founder, Stella & Dot

# Chapter Twelve

## OUR GO-TO SMARKETING STRATEGY

---

We've talked about our SMarketing strategy throughout this book. It's quickly become an integral part of our identity at Tulip Media Group and something we take immense pride in.

We went from having an inbound lead—someone calling us—maybe once a month to having qualified inbound leads coming in two to three times a day!

The objective of a powerful SMarketing strategy is to synthesize the roles of sales and marketing to increase the percentage of conversions achieved from inbound leads. The shift from a diverged, outbound selling model to an inbound model is comparable to changing your strategy from chiming into conversations out of turn (Erika, is that you again?) to being the center of the conversation. In effect, a SMarketing model is designed to open the door for customers who want what you're selling to come to you.

We implemented a SMarketing strategy for ourselves before we began selling it to our Client-Partners. This way, we can tell you that it's tried and true and produces phenomenal results for us and all of the Client-Partners we've brought on board. For many of our valued Client-Partners, a Tulip Media SMarketing strategy made the difference between fizzling out in the wake of the pandemic and feeding the flame. We couldn't be prouder to hold the spark that brought these businesses back to life.

We've become enamored with the process and the inspirational stories we get to hear from people who really do want to talk to us. A SMarketing system has also generated leads for us that we would have never pursued in an outbound marketing system. What we mean by this is that SMarketing opens the door for companies we wouldn't expect to use our services. We can now tailor a program for them and try something that might be just a little outside of our comfort zone with some amazing results.

On the selling side, we have heavily automated what used to be the role of several salespeople. Search engine optimization and pay-per-click advertising play an integral role in this.

With that said, we understand the importance of having that personal element, so we are careful to still integrate our human role throughout the process as needed. All new inquiries come in through our website, which is part of the SMarketing itself. In fact, we are utilizing a SMarketing strategy to generate the sales of our SMarketing product. Cool, right?

We want to show you what SMarketing looks like in action.

We no longer have a designated sales team and have not made a cold call since May 2019. Letting our team of seven dedicated salespeople go that somber afternoon was one of the hardest decisions we ever made, but it has made us stronger in the long run. Moving away from an outbound sales strategy was crucial to achieving the results we're seeing now. Our sales model now is completely inbound and thriving.

When your inquiries come in through our website, our production team jumps right in to answer any questions you as a potential Client-Partner might have. You also have the option to call us with inquiries during standard working hours. Because we serve Client-Partners across North America, we're available throughout the day and night to take your calls. Now that we are working from home full-time, taking your calls has never been easier. Our home offices are outfitted with everything we need to assist you, and we even have office numbers forwarded to our cellphones so we can cater to you while we're on the go.

Once we've persuaded you to come aboard as a Client-Partner, we'll explore in-depth the programs that would be effective for your purposes. Each of our program offerings is tailored to your needs and is compatible with our growing list of other program offerings.

Now that we've brought SMarketing into the heart of Tulip Media, all of our programs are designed to work with inbound selling and marketing systems. We've even created a dynamic pricing calculator to help you understand exactly where your marketing dollars are going. This also enables you to play around with your Tulip Media financial commitment in your free time to make sure we're adding the value you expect of us and more. We're always happy to meet with you to discuss our role in your company's long-term sales and marketing strategy.

The next stop in our working partnership is to get your first project on the go. This is the real time for us to shine for you. Once you give us the go-ahead, we are the ones that take all the responsibility for implementing the necessary measures to complete your first project from start to finish. Expect us to get creative here and rest assured that we'll wow you. Standing out is what we do best.

SMarketing focuses heavily around creating online content and designing an inbound sales model. The thing that makes SMarketing so easy for us is that we can actually integrate the writing services we offer straight into your SMarketing program. Any article we've written for your magazine can be seamlessly search engine optimized and uploaded to your blog to start driving traffic and conversions. In fact, we've actually started designing our magazine content with the SMarketing processes in mind. This means that you'll often find your magazine articles have already targeted a keyword phrase and have been optimized for generating online traffic without you knowing.

Because we have the most involvement in all parts of the process, we as production managers are generally the ones who answer the questions that come up. We have been doing this for many years, so we've immersed ourselves in a lot of different articles and strategies. Again, that's collective knowledge that we share with our entire team, but it's still important to acknowledge our own expertise when it comes to deciding who is the right person for the job.

This is a completely different approach from calling in and reaching a sales representative whose primary purpose is simply to sell a product. Outbound sales models tend to focus heavily on the positive aspects of a product and making the product fit the client, even where it may not be appropriate. Transparency and honesty are as important to us as Client-Partner satisfaction. We know everything there is to know about our products and processes so we can tell you in all honesty if we can add value for you and which products and services would be the best combination for your company.

We constantly practice our pitches with each other for accuracy and objections. Having spent many years in sales, Erika can attest to the increased effectiveness of a pitch by someone who works in production and delivers the service themselves. There's a huge advantage to operating this way, and we've really reaped the benefits, evident through a visible increase in sales and cohesion.

The only time that we've not hit our sales goal since adopting the SMarketing strategy was when the COVID-19 pandemic first hit. Other than that, every single quarter has surpassed our greatest expectations. During the pandemic, or "COVID quarter" as Stacey calls it, the inquiries did not necessarily go away; they just seemed to go on hold while existing and potential Client-Partners focused on rebuilding their own businesses internally. We still had potential Client-Partners inquiring about magazines and digital marketing. They just weren't ready to implement this strategy just yet. However, the COVID quarter did create a strong pipeline for our second and third quarters, which has pushed us back to the top in terms of sales targets. It's so satisfying to be achieving the sales we have with no sales team. Truly, we as a team have been just knocking it out of the park for conversions.

When we started using our SMarketing strategy for ourselves, the formula we created really astounded us all. Andy, our founder and CEO, belongs to several different coaching and mastermind groups. His sharing of our success in these groups alone generated a considerable amount of SMarketing sales for us. As it turns out, telling the story of how we went from having a designated sales team to none and accelerating growth has really resonated with fellow entrepreneurs and business leaders heading multi-million-dollar companies.

It was interesting to receive such a tremendous response to such an outside-the-box program. When we'd first looked into enacting rapid growth, we'd knocked down office walls and installed cubicle stations to make room for a new sales team we were sure would be the secret to becoming a multi-million-dollar company. This was the way other companies were doing it, after all. Having made such a commitment, making the decision to let all of them go within that same year was even harder than it would have been otherwise because we had believed in the outbound selling process so strongly at that point in time.

Letting an entire sales team go in one day stirred up a fuss in our industry. Other businesses were genuinely intrigued and eager to hear more about this program we called SMarketing. We immediately had people asking us to do the same for them.

Before we even released our SMarketing program officially, we had Client-Partners waiting for us to pull them aboard. To implement this most effectively for them, we developed a package and very quickly started selling it. We've hardly had to advertise at all. In fact, we only started advertising our SMarketing program after about a year of unprecedented success with existing Client-Partners.

It's neat to be able to see the difference our magazines and our newsletters make when we come out with a beautiful, finished product, but those results aren't instantaneous. While a professional magazine will generate leads over time as the issue is picked up by your target clients, a SMarketing strategy has the potential to produce results almost immediately.

One tweak here with keyword phrases and meta, then another one there in Google Ads can make all the difference for your funnel tomorrow. It's exciting to watch the process unfold for each Client-Partner with SMarketing and for Tulip Media as a whole. We have evolved so much from where we started, and we're really looking forward to growing and bringing more value to our Client-Partners.

"I noticed that the dynamic range between what an average person could accomplish and what the best person could accomplish was 50 or 100 to 1. Given that, you're well advised to go after the cream of the cream. A small team of A+ players can run circles around a giant team of B and C players."

— Steve Jobs, Co-Founder
Of Apple And Former CEO

# Chapter Thirteen

## LIVING OUR CULTURE

When we have someone, who has made it through the extensive interviewing and onboarding process and they are hired to join our team, we make them feel really special. The week before they start, we send flowers to their house as a welcoming gift and a gesture to let them know we're excited to have them. In advance of their first day, we buy their team jersey. On their first day, we prepare their desk with balloons and make reservations for a team lunch or takeout.

For each person we bring on, we set their computer up fully before they arrive. This means setting up all of the programs they will need, creating shortcuts and passwords for them, getting everything ready to go so they are set for success on the big day. There's nothing more frustrating than starting at a new company with a brand-new computer that isn't set up to perform any of the tasks you need to do. We work hard to eliminate this stress for our new team members.

For virtual hires, we emulate the same things through a welcome package that has everything they need to outfit their home office.

We set the tone of going completely above and beyond from day one. When they log in to that new computer, their Gmail, Salesforce, and Teamwork accounts are already set up and waiting for them. Now that we are working in a virtual world, we have a Google account created and set up that the new hire can simply link into from their devices. All of the work they do is automatically saved to our company drive.

They receive all of their business cards and a team jersey right away, complete with a custom caricature. The team jersey boasts the caricature on the front with the number hired on the back (for instance, Stacey was hired second, so her jersey is #2).

Because we don't take ourselves too seriously, everyone on our team uses a caricature in place of a formal business portrait. Although each character is still dressed in formal wear, this resonates with the lightheartedness of our culture and our brand.

Our characters represent us in a lot of the things that we do, which is another aspect of our culture that makes us stand out. Getting to know the people on our team for who they are is paramount. Reflecting these traits back in a caricature is a fun way to build cohesion.

Often, Andy spends the first half of the day with any new hire talking about our office culture and informally explains how our office works and how we work together. He also seizes the opportunity to better understand them as a person as he develops a better idea of how they will fit into our organizational structure.

Beyond our internal team, we work with outsourced writers, editors, designers, administrators, and more. These people assist us in very specific ways to fulfill niche needs of the many moving pieces we have within the organization.

Recently, we've started doing caricatures for our writers as well. Although they do not fill a full-time role on our team, it's important to us that these people know how seen and appreciated they are for all that they do. Maintaining the tone of our Client-Partners and meeting our tight deadlines is not easy work, after all.

In early 2020, one of our editors was scheduled to go to Japan. It had been quite a few years in the making, and he was so excited for him and his wife to vacation there for their 30th anniversary. Because of the pandemic, he chose not to go. We knew this was a huge blow for him, so we bought him a gift card to one of the local sushi restaurants in his area and had it mailed to him. We knew it wasn't the same as eating sushi in Japan, but we made it a priority to communicate that we sympathized with him and wanted to do a little something to lessen the blow.

We've made similar gestures for our proofreaders and video editors for significant life events that have come to our attention. Our culture is heavily based around the little things we do to make life that little bit better for everyone that we work with. In the bigger picture, all of these little things make a big impact.

We would like to think we have some effect on the cultures of our Client-Partners, too. Through our intimate role as a marketer and the ways we strategize, we often find ourselves in a position to influence. We fuel the fountain of pride that comes with effective marketing and cultivate ways for using it as a tool to gain traction and to build community.

Denise Lee Yohn talks a lot about culture. One of the things she explores is how a company's external brand is an extension of its internal culture and core values. Being the right fit for our company isn't just about practicing our core values internally. It's about alignment with how we live.

Everybody at Tulip Media lives our core values outside of work as well as throughout the workday, which is why we've all turned out to be such a great fit for our roles here. We want our Client-Partners to truly recognize who we are as people and our values.

One of the things we do is called Giftology as coined by John Ruhlin, the author of *Giftology*. John is a national contributor and friend to Tulip Media. He has many more unique and innovative ideas on how to gift effectively. We send out at least one gift a week because we love to show our appreciation. It could be for someone who assists us internally, someone who went above and beyond to do some really amazing work, or one of our valued Client-Partners. There are lots of reasons why we would send a gift. One thing is always true: we buy gifts we know others would love to receive.

There's a theory that if you send a gift and it has your logo on it, that's marketing. In order to be authentic, we brand all of our gifts with the name or the logo of the person or company we are sending the gift to. This makes it a true gift. That says, "It's not about me." It tells the receiver that the intention of the gift was to make them feel special, not to draw attention to ourselves. That's a really important message to send.

As an example, one time we were helping one of our Client-Partners secure a new client. To wow this potential client and the Client-Partner, we arranged to have a beautiful wooden box made with the receiver's logo engraved on the top of it. We then filled it full of their custom magazines and sent it out. This was purely for our Client-Partner because, as you now know, their success is our success. We use the tools available to us to help them.

We're all big fans of Yeti products and very often have these personally engraved as gifts. We love our own Yeti mugs, so we are always very confident that they will be well-received. We call this "Yeti Power."

Sometimes we get even more creative with our gifts. For one company, we helped design an animated logo for their company. We knew the design was going to be used for a sign, but we assumed it was for an electronic sign or something relatively small that would be displayed in their office. As it turns out, our design was made into a sign displayed at Gillette Stadium for the New England Patriots.

We have a few influencers that have been either national contributors or avid supporters. To show our appreciation for them, we've had bobbleheads created in their image. How unique a gift is that? It totally aligns with us taking our work very seriously but ourselves . . . not so much.

We once had a Client-Partner where all three owners of the company had wives that were expecting at the same time. As a gift, we bought them all onesies with their logo on them. This was a cute way to acknowledge that while their company was growing, so were their families.

We've done Cutco knives engraved with a family name. With a knife, chances are, you're going to go home and deposit it in the knife drawer, which is used by everyone in your family. We make sure to think about how a gift will be used when we're customizing the gift because that's a huge part of what makes it special. We like to get the family involved because it feels like we've contributed something to their personal life outside of the work environment.

When we rebranded from Carle Publishing to Tulip Media, we sent packages to everybody. These packages came in a bright red box with a red silk tulip. Inside each box was a video card with a personalized video. The video started with the Carle Publishing logo, which morphed into the Tulip Media logo, and then combined with the Client-Partner's logo. This illustrated the progression of Carle Publishing turning into Tulip Media and Tulip Media being partnered with their respective companies. Every single Client-Partner we had received one of these.

Giftology plays a crucial role in our external culture and branding, but it also fuels us internally. On the inside, we put a lot of work into maintaining our team culture, and the biggest part is that we all treat each other like family. We're conscious of each other's needs and constantly thinking of ways to be supportive and show appreciation.

When Jessica's baby was born, we sent her the most obnoxious six-foot-tall teddy bear that we addressed directly to her daughter, Emma. A day after she got home from the hospital, there was a knock at her door—the bear had arrived. We didn't tell her who it was from until she related the incident to us later, but we knew it would stand as a bold reminder to everyone in her household how excited we were to be a part of their growing family.

We are very supportive of maternity leave in general. When babies are born, we purchase onesies with a similar format to the team jerseys we all receive on our first day. The onesies come with the team name (family name) on the back and the employee number plus a half underneath.

Andy has even gone so far as to help employees out of financial difficulty, providing short-term loans when they are needed. Everybody may have a moment of crisis and unexpected expenses. When you are distracted because of something financially, it can adversely affect your work ethic and more. We believe that assisting people personally helps professionally as well. Besides, it's the right thing to do.

We, all of us, provide each other with ongoing support. We always grow as a team. Likewise, when someone learns something that we know could be very valuable to everybody else, we share it.

Simon Sinek talks about being a finite learner or an infinite learner. Finite learners see education as segmented and often university is the end point for these people. Sinek disagrees with creating a finite learning space, encouraging the process to become infinite instead.

As your company is constantly growing, so should your knowledge and the knowledge of everyone working within your company to help it grow. If you are working for Tulip Media, you will always be a student, and we believe this should apply to any workplace. There's always something to learn from new experiences, and there's always a better way to do things, especially as your organization expands.

Our constant state of learning applies to everything, from new computer programs to soft skills like emotional intelligence. Everything like that is very important to us. With our BetterBookClub subscription, we are paid to read books and to educate ourselves on any number of subjects as they relate to growing and managing our roles within the company.

We also have an awesome wellness program where Tulip Media pays for physical activity, such as a gym membership or fitness classes, to help with stress relief. Overall, this helps us feel and function better as people inside and outside our jobs.

For at-home office equipment, we have the best of the best of everything we need. We don't waste time when it comes to hardware being slow. If one of us needs something to make our work life easier, we jump right in and make it happen for that person. If a computer is on its last legs, we'll start shopping around right away and get a new one delivered as soon as possible. We prioritize having this ongoing support for everyone because it is one less thing to worry about when equipment starts to give us trouble.

In another example of ongoing support, Andy encouraged Erika to attend Toastmasters, which is an international public speaking organization. She's always had what we call the "Gift of Gab," but she'd never been formally trained to use it. Attending Toastmasters, she learned so much about valuable presentation skills and improving upon what she was already good at.

Going above and beyond to learn those amazing public speaking tips and tricks was an experience that really had an impact on her not just as the managing editor but as someone who can now use these skills in her everyday life. She was actually in the Toastmasters program for several years and won several awards during this time. She became president of the Fredericton Toastmasters and won a Triple Crown Award in 2019.

Having opportunities to learn firsthand from renowned thought leaders and speakers is something that makes our employment so meaningful and keeps us motivated. We are fortunate to have access to some of the most brilliant business minds for our continued personal and company growth.

The opportunity to write this book is another great example of the ways that we are supported to blossom in our day-to-day roles. Having this opportunity funded by the company has meant the world to us. It also communicates that our development and success as individuals is a company priority at the highest level.

From the time the idea was initially proposed to the finished product, we've been immensely supported by all of our team and partners to ultimately achieve success as published authors. The amount of positive influence this has had on our mind-set and careers is incredible. How many other companies are determined to make their employees best-selling authors?

We hope that understanding how we live in our culture every day will inspire others to look at company culture through a different lens. We've demonstrated the difference that employee empowerment can make in steering an organization to success. You can see that employees who are aligned and living a positive company culture are more satisfied and willing to go the extra mile every day.

"Make sure everybody in the company has great opportunities, has a meaningful impact and is contributing to the good of society."

— Larry Page, CEO of Google

# Chapter Fourteen

## CREATING YOUR ULTIMATE CULTURE

---

One of our thought leaders, contributors, and friends to Tulip Media is Jack Daly. Jack talks about your culture as being either by design or by default. This means you either make it happen or it happens on its own.

To illustrate this point, Jack uses a gardening metaphor. He describes your organization at first as a blank and open field. If the field is fertile, something is bound to grow whether you plant it or not. It's your choice to either let the field be overtaken by weeds or to cultivate a beautiful garden that fuels your organization forward.

The state of your organization all depends on the time and the effort that you put into it. If you want to cultivate a beautiful garden, it's going to take a dedication of time and a commitment of effort to get there. You can't just sit back and wait for your garden to grow, because we know that isn't going to happen. If you do this, you'll quickly wind up with a field full of weeds.

The difference in "by design" and "by default" is the action you take to consistently nurture the organizational environment. Note that this isn't going to be a one-and-done type of interaction. You aren't going to cultivate the garden once and reap the benefits forever, because that's not how gardening works. In order to continually benefit from the fruit of the garden—your ultimate culture—you will need to tend to it daily. You need to make sure all of its needs are being met and you are getting rid of all the weeds before they become bigger problems.

When you do nothing, the weeds—or negative culture—seize the opportunity to take over. This scenario will play out whether you've left the field blank to begin with or whether you've planted a beautiful garden and walked away. No matter what you've done to this point, as soon as you sit back and do nothing, you give negative culture the chance to set in.

Once you have planted the beautiful garden, you need to nurture it. This means you are going to make time each day to pull the weeds, give it some water, assess your plant health, maybe add a little bit of fertilizer. All of these things need to be done all of the time.

So, how do you nurture your garden and cultivate positive culture on an ongoing basis? You begin by defining your core values.

There's a *Harvard Business Review* article that features Jim Collins. In it, he talks about defining your culture in the context of the mission to Mars. The "Mission to Mars" exercise asks you to imagine that you are recreating the best version of your organization on another planet, but you only have room to take five to seven people. Who would you send and why?

The purpose of this exercise is to establish what you view as the most important fundamental values of your organization. The people you decide to send are likely to be exemplars of the organization's core values and purpose. They'll also have the highest level of credibility and the highest levels of competence among your team.

Pay close attention to why you choose who you do and what it is about them that makes them an ideal fit for your company's culture. What do they value that your organization also values prominently? Why are these shared values essential to the success of your organization as a whole?

While you're assessing who you would send, you should also be paying attention to those you've omitted from the mission.

We tend to always focus on the positive attributes that people have, but building a positive culture also requires that you consider the negative.

What about some of the employees that weren't a fit in this exercise? Think about the reasons why they weren't a fit.

You may find the ones you've kept on Earth are simply too mediocre. Maybe they aren't terrible employees, but there isn't really anything special about them either. Sometimes, there's more to it than that.

When you think about your all-time worst employees, usually there is one trait that jumps out more than others as to why they're not a fit for your culture. As much as you want to look for all the great attributes that people have, you also want to look for signs that maybe they're not a good fit.

It's interesting because those people who don't fit in your organization because of that one toxic trait are actually very much like weeds in your beautiful garden. Maybe those small shortcomings don't seem like much, but they can actually have an exponential impact on the behavior of your entire team.

Think back to those mediocre employees that you omitted from the mission. How might their behavior have changed if all of the employees around them had been shining examples of positive company culture and core values? Is it possible that the negative influences became an excuse not to give their all because they could see very clearly that not everyone was aligned?

Jim Collins talks about defining your core values and we talk about living your core values. As you now know, we at Tulip Media talk about a core value each morning before we start the workday. Part of this discussion is recognizing someone who completely embodied that core value. Whether it's something that happened this morning or this week, we are always providing examples of living our core values.

At this point, most of what we do is just second nature, but colleagues are consistently recognizing how each other's behavior relates to our core values. When the fit between employees and company is so compatible, living our core values really just comes down to making the most natural decision we would make for ourselves and our work family. It doesn't become a matter of not knowing what to do because we all trust that our personality and values are so aligned that we just need to do what comes naturally to us.

This takes the well-nurtured garden to another level. In our company garden, we've now got plants—or employees—that work together to keep the garden beautiful too.

We review our core values monthly and quarterly and award our core values trophy weekly. The person who received the trophy the previous week always has the honor of awarding it to the next person. This provides a great opportunity for the trophy holder to shine the spotlight on someone whose efforts may have gone unnoticed by the rest of the team. This could be someone they were working closely with that week on a project the rest of us weren't involved in yet, so we didn't get a chance to see how much they put into it.

For example, Erika might be working with Carmen on a magazine layout one week and know that the Client-Partner was really pleased with the layout she presented. No one else on the team will see the layout until completion two months later, but Erika can seize this opportunity to award the trophy to Carmen for going above and beyond to deliver a product the Client-Partner is proud of. Everyone on our team does amazing work, and it's important for us to find ways to acknowledge this wherever we can.

In your own organization, we highly recommend taking up a daily-huddle format and putting together some sort of recognition exercise that will highlight those doing an exemplary job of living the company values. It's easy to award the top salespeople for meeting targets, but what about those who go the extra mile to perform those smaller tasks daily? It's important to recognize everyone that is contributing to the company success and nurturing the beautiful garden you've created inside and out.

Our performance reviews are based 50 percent on our productivity or ability to do the job and 50 percent on living our core values. The core values portion is centered around trust, drive, reliability, communication, and a positive attitude towards change. You can replace the focal points of the assessment with whatever your core values are. Someone who fits completely within the company will share all of your core values, anyway. You will not have to force a perfect candidate to adopt any new behavior traits because their existing traits should already be compatible with the culture of your organization.

Assigning such a heavy portion of the performance review to each person's ability to live the company's core values means that anyone who isn't a good fit naturally won't last very long. If who they are, what they believe, the way they treat people, and the way they want to be treated themselves isn't consistent with our criteria, then that performance review will quickly weed them out.

Those employees who do live the core values every day will appreciate that they are being considered in a much bigger frame than simply their ability to perform in their role. They'll also be appreciative of having all of those little things they do for the organization be noticed and applauded by everyone else.

If someone is not living up to your core values, you must be willing to fire the offender. Having a weed growing in your organization will steal the light and nutrients away from your flowers and fruit-bearing plants. The fastest way to destroy your culture is to have someone in the middle ruining it.

You can spend months and months, even years, doing amazing things with your culture, but if you have someone at the center disrupting the rest of the team or not pulling their own weight, making other people frustrated, or blatantly disregarding core values, you can destroy your culture and everything that you worked for in a heartbeat.

In order to keep your team motivated and living to their highest potential, you need to keep the environment clean and beautiful. When someone doesn't live up to the core values, you really do need to remove them from the situation. Trust that a new hire will come along that is a better fit for the team.

In general, you must be willing to take a financial hit to live the core value. At Tulip Media, we were asked to do this a few years ago. We were going into a rough period, and we were all asked to take a 10%–20% decrease in our pay for three months.

In most organizations, this would result in at least some of the team walking away, but not for us. Andy talked to each of us individually and took our unique financial situations into account. Some of us were able to take more of a hit than others, but we all took the hit together and saw it through to the other side.

Why did we do this? Because we all believe in the values of this organization so wholeheartedly that we were willing to suffer in the short term to reap the benefits in the long term. When you love what you do, you are willing to make sacrifices.

This should never be something you expect your employees to do, but if the circumstance were to arise, would they be willing? Do they believe that strongly in the values of the organization that they would want to see it through to the other side?

Most of us on the Tulip Media team are also shareholders of the company, which illustrates how truly invested we are in seeing the company succeed. How many of your own employees are financially invested in your company? This figure speaks volumes about the alignment of your team with your company culture. Your organization should be more than just the place employees' clock in and clock out every day. Your company and your culture should be a way of life for everybody in it.

Our core values and the necessity of living them play a huge role in our onboarding messaging. In fact, one of the reasons we wrote this book was for when we need to hire more staff in the future. When we are recruiting new people, we need those new people to really understand our culture from the inside out. We thought this book would be helpful. Not only will other companies benefit from understanding what a positive and well-nurtured culture looks like in action, any potential candidates can quickly develop their knowledge of what it means to be a Tulip Media employee and how we embody our culture every single day.

You get much more out of your team when you have people coming together who enjoy what they do. When you take it upon yourself to create that environment of alignment and synergy within your organization, your team will truly be ready to take on the impossible.

When you've got everybody on the same team, when you've got everybody pulling together, when you've got aligned values, that's what makes the magic happen. What matters most for your culture can't be written on any piece of paper. It comes from the heart.

And that's why it's about DNA, not resume.

"We believe that it's really important to come up with core values that you can commit to. And by commit, we mean that you're willing to hire and fire based on them. If you're willing to do that, then you're well on your way to building a company culture that is in line with the brand you want to build."

— Tony Hsieh, CEO Of Zappos

# ABOUT THE AUTHORS

Left: Stacey O'Brien, right: Erika MacLeod

# ABOUT THE AUTHORS
## Erika MacLeod

Erika came to work for Tulip Media in early 2015. She was initially part of the sales team but later moved into account management and ultimately landed the role of managing editor that she so "eloquently" performs today. Erika graduated from the University of New Brunswick in 2001 with a double major in Psychology and Law in Society.

From being high school president to committee leader in university to spending summers on the softball field to being former president of the local Toastmasters Chapter, Erika has always been involved in the community, which reflects her social nature. As a social butterfly, Erika adores having a job that enables her to show her best side always through interaction with peers and engaging with thought leaders and Client-Partners.

Erika is excited to add her voice to the growing community of thought leaders that are transforming the curation of culture in the workplace and beyond. Erika resides in Fredericton, New Brunswick, with pit bull rescue, Georgia, affectionately named after her roots.

---

**Favorite Quotes –**

**"I want every little girl who's told she's bossy, to be told instead she has leadership skills"** – Sheryl Sandberg

**"She believed she could, so she did!"** – RS Grey

# ABOUT THE AUTHORS
## Stacey O'Brien

Stacey comes to Tulip Media from a long career in owning and managing restaurants. For 20 years, she thrived in this fast-paced, multi-level environment. Prior to coming to Tulip Media Group in 2013, Stacey owned and operated five franchise restaurants. Stacey graduated from college twice, with diplomas in both Accounting and Entrepreneurial Management. Stacey is Tulip founder Andy Buyting's eyes and ears in the digital office. She assists with everything from the company bookkeeping, human resources, and office management to project and property management. Her diverse and extensive management experience equipped Stacey well for the many hats she wears in the dynamic work environment alongside the rest of Team Tulip.

As the second employee that Andy hired at Tulip Media, Stacey's interview process is still a topic of laughter in the office; however, the Shackleton method did ensure she was a good fit to keep everything on the company ship running smoothly. Stacey's official title is VP of Everything, which suits her role to a tee because there's no way someone could list all of the diverse task and scenarios she handles on the day-to-day.

In her spare time, Stacey likes to stay on the move with large-scale projects inside and outside of work. Her hobbies include buying and renting homes, Airbnb host, and bookkeeping for a variety of businesses. Stacey resides at home with daughter Haley, partner Brian, and two dogs, Cora and Lucy. Some of her hobbies include spending time at her cottage, exploring back roads, and enjoying the outdoors through kayaking, ATVs, and a nice glass of wine.

**Favorite Quote –**

**"If you look at what you have in life, you'll always have more. If you look at what you don't have in life, you'll never have enough."** – Oprah Winfrey

CPSIA information can be obtained
at www.ICGtesting.com
Printed in the USA
BVHW091235300621
610532BV00005B/16